LAOS
CAMBODIA

SAY IT IN LAOTIAN

ENGLISH	*LAOTIAN*
Good morning, good day	*Sabaidee*
How are you?	*Sabaidee bo?*
Well, thank you	*Sabaidee, kop chai*
Goodbye	*La koon*
Yes/No	*Tyao or Euh / Bo*
What is your name?	*Jao seu nyang*
My name is…	*Koy sou…*
I do not understand	*Koy bo kao chai*
Please	*Kaloona*
Thank you	*Kop chai*
Excuse me…	*Ko tot*
Help!	*Suay dae!*
Where is…?	*… you sai?*
…hotel	*Hong hem*
…bank	*Bhanakaan*
…post office	*Paisani*
…market	*Talaat*
…hospital	*Hong mo*
…restaurant	*Han ahan*
How much?	*Tao dai?*
I need a doctor	*Koy tong kan ha mo*
Where are the toilets?	*Hong suam you sai?*
Today	*Meu ni*
Tomorrow	*Meu eun*
Aeroplane	*Hua bin*
Boat	*Hua*
Bus	*Lot may*
Bicycle	*Lot thip*
Motorcycle	*Lot chak*
Do you have a room?	*Mi hong wang bo?*
Mosquito net	*Mung*
Drinking water	*Nam doom*

Contents

Vietnam   1

Laos   73

Cambodia   105

Fold-out maps

Vietnam

Laos, Vientiane, Luang Prabang

Cambodia, Angkor, Phnom Penh

SAY IT IN KHMER

ENGLISH	KHMER
Good morning, good day	*Chum riap*
Hello	*Sua sadai*
How are you?	*Niak sohk sabai de?*
Well, thank you	*Knom sohk sabai*
Goodbye	*Li ahs*
Yes	*Baat* (for men), *Ja* (for women)
No	*Tay*
What is your name?	*Niak chmuah ei?*
My name is…	*Knom cmaah…*
I do not understand	*Tee knom min yaal tee*
Please	*Soum*
Thank you	*Ar koun*
Excuse me…	*Suomto*
Help!	*Juay knom phwang*
How can I get to…?	*Phleuv naa teuv…?*
…hotel	*Santakea*
…bank	*Thniakia*
…post office	*Bprai sa nee*
…market	*Psaa*
How much?	*Ponman?*
What is this called?	*Nnih ke hav thaa mait?*
I need a doctor	*Juay hav krou paet mao*
Where are the toilets?	*Bongkohn neuv ai naa?*
Today	*Thngay nih*
Tomorrow	*Thngay saik*
Aeroplane	*Yaun hawh*
Bus	*Lan thom*
Car	*Roteh lan*

PHOTO CREDITS
Hémisphères/Verdeil, R. Holzbachovà

VIETNAM

**Bernard Joliat
and
Sonia Vian**

JPMGUIDES

Contents

This Way Vietnam   **3**

Flashback   **7**

On the Scene   **17**

    The North   **17**

    The Centre   **31**

    The South   **51**

Shopping   **59**

Dining Out   **61**

Sport and Entertainment 63

The Hard Facts   **64**

Index   **72**

Maps

Hanoi	69
Hué	70
Ho Chi Minh City	71

Fold-out map

Vietnam

This Way Vietnam

Welcoming Land

Content to have shaken off colonialism and the deprivations of hardline socialism, Vietnam has taken significant steps towards a market economy by opening its frontiers to tourism, trade and investment. Though it was weakened by the long and painful war of independence, the country is slowly recovering its freedom of expression. In Asia this means, first and foremost, the right to do business. Cheerful faces bear witness to a new-found optimism.

The Vietnamese say that the map of their country resembles the bamboo pole with huge baskets balanced at each end that they use to carry goods to market. One basket represents the Red River delta, the other the Mekong delta. Bordered on the north and the west by China, Laos and Cambodia, and open to the Gulf of Tonkin and Nam Hai (South China Sea) on the east, Vietnam covers a land area of 329,566 sq km (127,246 sq miles)—almost as large as Germany. This long, narrow strip of land, in places no more than 50 km (31 miles) wide, has a population of more than 80 million.

Geographically, the country covers three great regions. In the north lies the capital, Hanoi, with 3 million inhabitants, at the heart of the fertile Red River delta—also known as Tonkin. The mountainous terrain of the centre, Annam, is dominated by the port of Danang and the ancient imperial capital of Hué. The wide delta of the Mekong in the south (Cochin China) embraces Ho Chi Minh City—the former Saigon—today Vietnam's most populous city with 5 million inhabitants.

The Vietnamese people proper, who live mostly in the plains and the urban centres, make up the country's largest ethnic group (85 per cent of the population), with 53 cultural minorities scattered along the border regions.

Mountains and plateaux cover three-quarters of the country. The lowlands form a green patchwork quilt stitched together by rivers and canals. Offshore are thousands of islands. The highest peak is the 3,143-m (10,312-ft) Fan Si Pan (or Hoang Lien Son) in the north.

The Essentials

Careful planning will enable you to see in a fortnight the best of the countryside and a fair share of the cultural attractions of this amazing country. A first visit ought to 3 include most of the essential sites of the cities and the coast—Hanoi, Ha Long Bay, Hué, Danang, Hoi An, Nha Trang, Dalat, Ho Chi Minh City and the Mekong delta—with perhaps an excursion to meet some of the varied ethnic groups who live in the mountainous border regions.

Ho Chi Minh City

Life in Ho Chi Minh City (the former Saigon) is light-hearted, trundling along at the same speed as its millions of bicycles and motorcycles, though the numbers of cars are ever increasing. In contrast to the street life of China, the atmosphere here is carefree, chaotic and exuberant. Unless you are filled with nostalgia for colonial days, it will not be the stately buildings lining the streets of Saigon that leave the most lasting impressions, but rather the frenetic lifestyle of the people.

Never keen to comply with the rules of collectivism, stall-holders are now doing more business than ever, cleverly salvaging and recycling anything that comes their way, creating desirable goods out of items you would probably have thrown into the bin without a second thought.

Two hours from Ho Chi Minh City, the small city of My Tho is reached by way of a scenic road bordered by paddy fields, fruit trees and orchids. Bathed in an indefinable light, the city is linked by waterways to the immense Mekong delta. From each of the cities on the nine channels of this great river, boats transport their passengers to the floating markets or tropical gardens, and into scenes straight out of the film *The Lover*, inspired by Marguerite Duras's novel which was partly based on her own life.

Northeast of the bustle of Ho Chi Minh City, in pleasant hill country, the town of Dalat, at an altitude of 1,475 m (4,839 ft), offers a different aspect of Vietnam. The daily market here is the meeting place of the various ethnic minorities of this refreshing wooded region, dotted with lakes and waterfalls.

The Centre

Nha Trang and its neighbouring islands form a beautiful coastal resort, the ideal place to relax after a journey along the Mandarin Road. Opportunities for water sports are wide-ranging here, and the seafood will delight everyone whose mouth starts watering at the thought of the coast.

Danang, in the centre of the country, boasts a fine museum devoted to the Cham culture, good preparation for an excursion to My Son, the capital and intellectual and religious centre of the ancient kingdom of Champa. In nearby Hoi An, UNESCO has listed almost 850 buildings of importance to Vietnam's cultural heritage.

North of Danang, in the imperial city of Hué, you'll encounter some of Vietnam's most beautiful historic sites, legacies of the long line of Nguyen rulers. Situated on the Perfume River, Hué (once known as Phu Xuan) mingles the romance of its serene landscapes with the splendour of a bevy of palaces, pavilions and tombs.

Hanoi and Ha Long Bay

In Hanoi, the Mot Cot (One Pillar) Pagoda and the Temple of Literature go back almost a thousand years. There are pagodas to please every taste in the city and the surrounding area. But Vietnam's past can also be explored in the Museum of History, the Museum of the Revolution and the Museum of the Army, which have become places of pilgrimage for France's Indochina combatants and American Vietnam War veterans, as well as the Vietnamese themselves. And you don't need to be a veteran to feel the atmosphere at the many battlefield sites, where so many lives were lost.

From Hanoi, you can explore Ha Long Bay, where junks and sampans navigate their way skilfully around a dreamland of 3,000 tropical islets and limestone reefs, a natural landscape that has been described as the eighth wonder of the world.

Having seen all this, you will surely want to make a second trip, to soak up the timeless atmosphere that's present in every aspect of the country, from the savoury cuisine, the arts, landscapes and festivals, down to the very fragrances wafting in the air. You have to experience the accidental, the spontaneous and the unexplained—the Vietnam you will discover by delving deeper is even more fascinating.

1

THE MOST BEAUTIFUL BAY The 3,000 islets of **Ha Long Bay** surge high up from the waters, forming a bizarre aquatic labyrinth of craggy rocks in astounding shapes. According to legend, the gigantic sculptures were created by a dragon who threw himself into the sea from his lofty lair, creating a network of fissures in the rocks below. When the sea rolled back after the cataclysm, it submerged all but the highest parts, which now compose a breathtaking wonderland.

Flashback

The First Dynasties

The Vietnamese people (the Kinh), the largest ethnic group in the country, claim to be the children of Au Co, who sat on a hundred eggs and hatched as many giants. The eldest of these, in 2879 BC, supposedly inaugurated the mythical dynasty of the Hung, whose 18 kings ruled over Van Lang, a kingdom in the Red River delta, until 257 BC. This kingdom was to become Vietnam.

At the end of the second millennium BC, bronze was brought by one of the last waves of Indonesian immigrants to the delta. Its arrival contributed to the rise of the Dong Son culture that was already established at this crossroads of Annam (central Vietnam) and Yunnan (south China). It evolved to a relatively high level, assimilating the influences of its Indonesian forebears with Mongoloid strains from incursions of Viet and Tai peoples. Further development was encouraged from the 4th century BC onwards, by turning the Red River delta marshland into an expanse of paddy fields.

Preparations for Tet, the Vietnamese New Year.

Under the Thuc dynasty, (257–207 BC), the future Vietnam called itself Au Lac. Under Trieu rule (207–111 BC), it was known as Nam Viet and controlled much of southern China, but the situation was reversed when the powerful Han rulers of China conquered the region.

Chinese Domination

Under the Han dynasty, the country was known as Giao-Chi until AD 203. The story of the famous "Trung sisters' revolt" (AD 39–43) has been handed down over the ages. The sisters, widows of local aristocrats, led an uprising against Chinese rule. The revolt was briefly successful, and the older sister, Trung Trac, set herself up as ruler of an independent state. But a Chinese counteroffensive ended in the defeat of the Vietnamese—and the suicide of the Trung sisters.

Chinese domination of the Red River delta continued until the 10th century. Although the Vietnamese were never reconciled to Chinese rule, Confucianism and Taoism won over the population, and the medical knowledge of the Buddhists compensated for the tyranny of the administration. In 678 the inexorable expansion of 7

Vietnam began when the Chinese annexed a region south of Tonkin, naming it Annam, "Dominion of the South".

The Hindu Kingdoms

From the 1st century AD, the south of today's Vietnam belonged to the Hindu kingdom of Funan (or Phu Nam), which participated in the lively exchange of trade and artistic and religious traditions between East and West. Contacts were wide-ranging—a Roman medallion of gold struck in 152 AD and bearing a likeness of the Roman Emperor Antoninus Pius has been found at Oc-Eo, Funan's chief port in the western part of the Mekong delta. In the 6th century, Funan proved unable to resist the attacks of the pre-Angkorian kingdom of Chen La, and was annexed to this powerful Cambodian empire.

During the same period, another Hindu kingdom, that of Champa, occupied the centre of the country (the region of Danang as its heartland) from the end of the 2nd century. This kingdom gradually expanded south as far as Phan Rang, leaving in its wake some monumental examples of its stunning art and architecture.

The First Vietnamese State

In 938, the Vietnamese commander Ngo Quyen took advantage of the collapse of the T'ang dynasty to push the Chinese back to the north. The battle of Bach Dang River ended 1,000 years of Chinese occupation and won independence for Vietnam. The reign of the Ngo dynasty was short-lived, however, as at the death of Ngo Quyen (965), General Dinh Bo Lynh seized power. His Dinh successor was in turn dethroned by Le Hoan, who proclaimed himself emperor under the name of Le Dai Hanh. His dynasty is called the Earlier Le.

The succeeding Ly dynasty (1010–1225), founded by Ly Thai To, consolidated the kingdom of Dai Viet. In this period the first Vietnamese university, the Temple of Literature in Hanoi, was inaugurated. Meanwhile, the Chinese were still smarting over their defeat and launched several attacks against Vietnam, but each time they were repulsed by the strategy of Ly Thuong Kiet (1030–1105). This national hero also had to contend with vigorous offensives from the south by the Cham and the Khmer. In the end, the Vietnamese won the day, conquering and pillaging Champa.

In 1225, the Ly dynasty was overthrown by the Tran, who, like their predecessors, improved the irrigation of the Red River delta. Remarkably, they also repelled the Mongols who had conquered China as well as most of the rest of Asia.

Cham monuments like these at Po Klong Garai are reminders of the Hindu kingdom which reached its height in the 15th century.

Tonkin's Robin Hood

In 1371, the Cham regrouped to pillage Hanoi. In this time of crisis, Ho Qui Ly usurped the throne from the Tran in 1400, only to see the Ming Chinese reappear in an explosion of extortion and brutality against the local people in 1406. A rich landowner, Le Loi, founded a centre of resistance in the village of Lam Son (Thanh Hoa Province) and fought the Chinese on behalf of the poor. He was a fair-minded man and prohibited pillage, thus becoming a much-admired local hero. The Chinese wanted to take advantage of his popularity and make him a mandarin, but this "Robin Hood of Tonkin" refused the honour, crushing the Chinese troops in 1427 and proclaiming himself Emperor of the Dynasty of the Later Le, under the name of Le Thai To. That year marks the true birth of Vietnam, which, liberated from Chinese cultural domination, went on to forge its own national identity and impose its rule on other territories. The Cham later became the victims of the Nam Tien, the "Great March South". The capital of Champa, Vijaya (Binh Dinh) fell to the Vietnamese in 1471.

The dynasty of the Later Le maintained its vigour until 1524, but continued to reign nominally 9 until 1778. In fact, real power was shared by the Trinh family in the north and the Nguyen in the south, who effectively ran the country between them.

The First Europeans

The first Europeans to set foot on Vietnamese soil were Portuguese sailors, who disembarked at Danang in 1516. The Nguyen lords put to use the weapons brought by the foreigners, invading the Mekong delta and defeating the Khmer. By the 17th century, Cambodia was finally obliged to recognize the sovereignty of Vietnam.

The Portuguese had come to do business. They established a trading post at Faifo (Hoi An) with the Japanese and the Chinese, while the Dutch installed themselves in the north. Missionaries flocked in from all over. The credit for inventing *quoc ngu*, the phonetic adaptation of the Roman alphabet to the Vietnamese language, used today by the Vietnamese, belongs chiefly to the French Jesuit priest Alexandre de Rhodes (1591–1660). Most European merchants left the country towards the end of the 17th century, but the missionaries put down roots in Vietnam: the erudition displayed by the Jesuits seduced the imperial court.

The Nguyen Dynasty

In 1777, three Tay-Son brothers from the south revolted against their rulers, pitting their forces first against the Nguyen and then the Trinh. By 1773 the Tay-Son held the centre of the country, and within fifteen years their dynasty had replaced the Le. Saigon and the Mekong delta fell into their hands in 1783. After taking refuge in Siam, 15-year-old Prince Nguyen Anh, the sole survivor of the fallen houses, reconquered the Mekong delta. With the financial support of a French bishop and French military advisers, he captured the Tay-Son stronghold in 1799 and the town of Hué in 1801. The following year, in Hué, the prince took the name of Gia Long and became emperor of the unified country, which he called Vietnam. He was the first of 13 Nguyen monarchs, a dynasty that ended only in 1945 when Bao Dai abdicated after the defeat of Japan and the success of the Vietminh.

Throughout their long reign, from 1802 to 1945, the Nguyen emperors supported the development and unity of the nation. Gia Long himself established citadels, dikes and lines of communication, notably the Mandarin Road between Saigon and China. But he was familiar with the ways of Westerners and advised his successor, Minh Mang (1820–40), to be wary of them. A fervent supporter of Confucian culture, the new emperor rejected "barbarian" influences. Eventually, rebellions broke out all over the country and it closed its doors to foreigners. But they were not to give in without a struggle.

French Colonization
British victory in the first "opium war" in 1842 opened Chinese markets to Europeans, but the emperors in Hué did not take much notice and continued their actions against foreigners, exe-cuting missionaries and murder-ing Vietnamese Catholics. This gave the Europeans a pretext for intrusion, and in August 1858 a fleet of 14 French and Spanish ships captured Danang. Saigon fell a short time later, and colonial forces took possession of the three provinces of Cochin China. In 1862 Emperor Tu Duc was forced to sign a treaty acknowl-edging this conquest, thus guar-anteeing foreign vessels access to his ports and granting missionar-ies free rein.

French presence spread to the centre and north of the country, and in 1883 Tonkin became a French protectorate, followed by Annam a year later. The Union of Indochina was created in 1887, uniting Cochin China, Tonkin, Annam, Laos and Cambodia. However, the triumph of the Chinese republicans under Sun Yatsen in 1911 and the defeat of Russia by the Japanese did much to encourage the nationalist senti-ments of the Vietnamese. French rule became more repressive; nat-ural resources were exploited while health and education were neglected.

The Republic
Nguyen That Thanh, the son of a mandarin born in 1892, visited London and the USA as a young man and lived in France from 1918, where he was a founder

member of the Communist Party. This was Ho Chi Minh. In 1925 he assembled followers in the Thanh-nien, the embryonic Vietnamese Communist Party. Later, his disciples founded the League for Vietnamese Independence, the Vietminh, which would one day spread terror among foreign military forces.

The Japanese invaded Vietnam in 1940 but left the French to govern for a while before deciding to take over themselves in March 1945. However, Japan's ambitions were annihilated in August when atomic bombs were dropped on Hiroshima and Nagasaki. Ho Chi Minh seized the moment; his August Revolution gave him control over the north and the centre of the country. In September 1945, he proclaimed the independence of the Democratic Republic of Vietnam.

The Fall of Dien Bien Phu

After World War II, France wanted to re-establish colonial rule and re-occupied most of the south, while Chinese Nationalist forces moved into the north. France negotiated the departure of the Chinese and then, in March 1946, signed agreements which confirmed Vietnam's independence, recognized by China and the Soviet Union. Limited numbers of French troops were to stay, but there would be a phased withdrawal, and a referendum in the south. But France did not respect the agreements. During the eight-year Indochina war that followed, 36,000 French soldiers were killed and almost 50,000 wounded. Casualties among the Vietnamese were even heavier. In May 1954, after nearly two months of heroic defence, 10,000 exhausted French soldiers surrendered at Dien Bien Phu to Vietnamese forces led by General Vo Nguyen Giap, while most of northern Vietnam and Laos fell into the hands of the Vietminh. The following day, the Geneva Conference began, and eight weeks later the war in Indochina was ended.

The Conference provided that Vietnam be divided in two at the Ben Hai River, near the 17th parallel. The territory north of this line of demarcation became the (communist) Democratic Republic of Vietnam led by President Ho Chi Minh. Free movement of people between north and south was guaranteed for 300 days. Almost a million refugees, most of them Catholic, fled the north and settled in South Vietnam, under the leadership of Ngo Dinh Diem, who declared himself President of the Republic of South Vietnam following a sham referendum. The United States closed the American consulate in Hanoi.

Pillaged over and over again, the imperial city of Hué still symbolizes the might of the Nguyen emperors.

The Vietnam War

In 1960, Vietminh supporters in the South formed the National Liberation Front (NLF)—disparagingly called the Vietcong—and launched effective guerilla attacks against the Diem regime. The North decreed general mobilization, demanding reunification of the country and withdrawal of all military forces. With progressive infiltration by the army of the North (the NVA), coming along the "Ho Chi Minh Trail" through Laos to support the Vietcong raids, South Vietnam found itself in danger of collapse. Perceiving a threat to other non-communist nations of the region (the "domi-no" effect), the Americans decided to intervene and sent in advisors and military aid. They provoked the overthrow of Ngo Dinh Diem on November 1, 1963. A succession of coups was to follow, eventually bringing Nguyen Van Thieu to power in 1967.

Meanwhile, the war had escalated. The first American combat troops landed at Danang in March 1965; by the end of the year they numbered 185,000. Two years later, there were almost half a million Americans and 800,000 other troops, mostly South Vietnamese but also Australians, Filipinos and South Ko-

13

reans. Bombing raids were launched against North Vietnam, and vast areas of the South were sprayed from the air with defoliants, to deprive the Vietcong and NVA of cover.

The US Pulls Out

In early 1968, the US base at Khe Sanh was attacked by NVA forces. This was a prelude to the Tet offensive which shook the entire American nation. On January 30, a hundred Vietcong commando raids were launched on the towns of the South, including Saigon, where the American ambassador escaped the surprise attack on his embassy by the skin of his teeth. After ten days of desperate fighting the communists were repulsed, but the psychological victory had given them encouragement. It also awakened the American conscience and international public opinion, traumatized by this pointless war. The newly elected President Nixon promised to work for peace and gradually reduced US troop numbers, but intensified the bombardment. Ho Chi Minh died in 1969 and so never saw the end of the war.

The peace talks that had begun in Paris in 1968 finally ended in an agreement in January 1973. The United States withdrew all its forces, leaving behind a gigantic store of military hardware for its allies in the South. But once again, agreements were not respected: President Nguyen Van Thieu broke the cease-fire and fighting began once more.

In January 1975, the North Vietnamese army crossed the 17th parallel and entered Saigon on April 30, nine days after the flight of Thieu. The Americans evacuated their embassy in total disarray. The two Vietnams were finally unified in July 1976 as the Socialist Republic of Vietnam.

Isolation

In 30 years of conflict, the country lost 3 million people, while 5 million more were mutilated. The government rebuilt the economy and strengthened its hold through strict, hard-line socialism. This led to political, religious and intellectual repression in the South, with offenders sent to "re-education" camps. From 1978, almost a million refugees fled Vietnam, mainly by sea in anything that would float, no matter how flimsy. Many of these "boat people" perished in the attempt; the survivors settled in the USA, Canada, Europe and Australia.

Backed by China, Pol Pot's Khmer Rouge attacked Vietnam in 1977. Strongly supported by the Soviet Union, the Vietnamese retaliated, took Cambodia and overthrew Pol Pot, installing a puppet sympathizer. The United States used this as an excuse to impose an embargo on Vietnam. In its turn, on the pretext of teaching Vietnam a lesson, China invaded several northern provinces in February 1979, but was again pushed out.

Opening Up

The withdrawal of Vietnamese forces from Cambodia after 1989 opened an era of détente in relations with the West and China. The Peace Treaty signed in October 1990 in Paris consolidated this reconciliation. The break-up of the Soviet Union in the 1990s and progressive withdrawal of the Russians from Vietnam accelerated reform. The

defection of its communist "allies" encouraged Vietnam to adopt a policy of popular capitalism assimilated into a socialist state. The reciprocal lifting of the American embargo in February 1994 permitted diplomatic and commercial relations between the two countries to resume. In 1995 Vietnam joined ASEAN, the Association of South-East Asian Nations.

Today, the wind of freedom is blowing across the country. Visitors are welcomed, including former refugees returning to see relatives or investigating investment opportunities. Tourism is one of the beneficiaries of this new outlook on the world.

On the Scene

Abounding in natural and cultural wonders, Vietnam generously rewards travellers in search of authenticity. With the opening up to tourism, comfortable hotels in line with Western standards have popped up all over the country, both in towns and at the historic sites.

From the Chinese frontier to the Mekong delta, you are free to travel anywhere you please. But in a country ravaged by 30 years of war, much of the road network is still in poor condition, despite major schemes for improvement. The main attractions are easy to reach, but if you want to see places off the beaten track, often more gratifying, you should be prepared to invest a little more time and money.

▶ THE NORTH

Hanoi, Excursions from Hanoi, From Hanoi to Ha Long, Ha Long Bay, The North

Hanoi

By setting up his capital in Thang Long, the City of the Soaring Dragon—today's Hanoi—Emperor Ly Thai To provided the independent kingdom of Dai Viet (Vietnam) with an ideal cultural site at the heart of Tonkin. Among Hanoi's three hundred buildings of interest, two of the most famous monuments date from his era—the One Pillar Pagoda (Chua Mot Cot), and the Temple of Literature (Van Mieu). But first, look around the Old Town and the lakes, and save some time for the museums.

Long Bien Bridge

Visitors flying into Hanoi have to cross the Chuong Duong Bridge, built with help from the Soviet Union and inaugurated in 1985. Before it was built, the only bridge taking traffic across the Red River into Hanoi was Paul

The best way to get around town is by cycle-rickshaw.

Doumer Bridge, now renamed Long Bien. American bombs destroyed the iron bridge, which carried road and rail traffic as well as pedestrians and cyclists. Following restoration, this symbol of colonial days was reopened to light traffic in 1984.

Old Town

Nestling between the citadel and Hoan Kiem lake, the old town of Hanoi is a picturesque compendium of colonial architecture, ancient communal houses *(dinh)*, Chinese shops and workshops, pagodas and hidden temples. Indulge in the charming atmosphere, the lively and colourful street scenes and some unusual shopping. In this area you'll also find some of the most sophisticated restaurants in Hanoi, serving a range of Vietnamese and Asian specialities.

Many of the lanes *(pho)* have retained the names of the traders' guilds that were located here, or of the merchandise which was traded: Rice Street, Silk Street, Cloth Street, Paper Street, Oil Street, and so on.

To the east of this area, the Independence Museum explores modern history.

Ho Hoan Kiem

Most of Hanoi's sanctuaries are built around a legend. The story associated with the Lake of the Restored Sword, in the heart of the city, goes back to the 15th century when the Chinese occupied the country. A golden turtle living in the lake gave to one Le Loi, a local fisherman, a sword which he used to put the invaders to flight. Le Loi was made emperor and returned the sword to the turtle.

The Temple of the Jade Mountain (Den Ngoc Son) stands on an islet near the north shore of the lake and is reached by crossing over the delicate little Bridge of the Rising Sun (The Huc).

Hoan Kiem lake is the setting for Hanoi's water puppet theatre; a performance of this delightful art form should not be missed.

Citadel and Army Museum

All that remains of the sturdy citadel built during Gia Long's reign, at the beginning of the 19th century, is the Flag Tower (Cot Co), some 60 m (197 ft) high, and now the symbol of Hanoi. It looms over the Army Museum, whose courtyard is filled with military paraphernalia, tanks, planes and artillery. Inside, the displays document various struggles for independence, such as the Battle of Dien Bien Phu.

Van Mieu

In 1070, emperor Ly Thanh Tong dedicated a Temple of Literature to Confucius. Six years later it became the first university in Vietnam, a centre for Confucian philosophy and morality, originally reserved for the sons of mandarins and nobles.

The building was modelled along the lines of the temple of Qufu, the birthplace of Confucius, in China. An astonishing succession of doors, courtyards, pavilions and sanctuaries fill a walled enclosure 350 m (1,148 ft) in length and 60–75 m (197–246 ft) wide. The inscription at the entrance requests visitors to dismount before entering.

The central doors and aisles were reserved for the emperor, the side aisles for the mandarins and the military.

The Pavilion of the Khué Van Constellation opens onto the third courtyard, whose delightful architectural details are reflected in the Thieu Quang Tinh (Well of Celestial Light). Around the square basin, 82 stone turtles bearing stelae (originally there were 117) date from 1484 to 1779. What, you may wonder, do the inscriptions record? The answer: exam results—names of the successful candidates for coveted positions in the imperial civil service. In the fourth courtyard, the sanctuaries were destroyed in 1946, but

WATER PUPPETS

Water puppet shows—known as Mua Roi Nuoc—are specific to the Red River region. Dating from the 11th century, they had almost become a forgotten art. Fortunately, when the tourist industry started to develop, the people took stock of their culture and saved this unique entertainment from oblivion.

The actors are painted wooden puppets that move about on a pool, accompanied by an orchestra playing in the background, in full view of the audience. The puppeteers, hidden behind a curtain or a bamboo screen, stand waist-deep in water to manipulate their tiny subjects, which represent villagers and their farm animals, kings, warriors and mythical beasts such as the phoenix, dragon and unicorn. Each satirical drama comprises several tableaux inspired by important topics such as great battles against the invader, the exploits of former kings, ancient legends, as well as the more mundane events of daily life. Singing, music and exploding fireworks underline the critical points of these enchanting fables.

The Hanoi theatre's repertoire is exceptionally varied. Outside the capital, several travelling groups wander up and down the country, putting on shows during festival periods.

two traditional temples remain, dedicated to the cult of Confucius.

Chua Mot Cot

According to legend, Ly Thai To longed for a male heir. After a dream in which the goddess Quan Am offered him a small boy, he hastened to marry a pretty country girl, who soon gave birth to a son. As a symbol of his gratitude, he had the curious One Pillar Pagoda built in 1049. Entirely made of wood, it survived undamaged for almost 1,000 years, only to be destroyed by the French when they abandoned the city in 1954. Restored, but with a concrete pillar replacing the original wooden one, the lotus-shaped pagoda emerges from the middle of a lotus pond.

Mausoleum of Ho Chi Minh

Opened in 1975 during the period of Vietnamese reunification, the mausoleum stands north of Chua Mot Cot in Badinh Square, where the Independent Republic of Vietnam was declared in 1945.

The father of Vietnamese independence lies in a glass coffin in the air-conditioned hall, contrary to his wish to be cremated. For two months every year, the body is sent to Moscow for a little cosmetic restoration.

Next to the mausoleum is a wooden house on stilts, which Ho Chi Minh had built for himself. A short walk further north is the sumptuous Presidential Palace, former residence of the French Governor General of Indochina, which Ho spurned for a more austere lifestyle.

Walking around this area you will see some of the most luxurious villas of the colonial era.

More lakes

Further north, beyond the sports stadium, is Ho Truc Bach. The

THE TWO MOST UNUSUAL TEMPLES At Tay Ninh, northwest of Ho Chi Minh City, the **Holy See of the Caodaists** is a shining example of religious eclecticism. Deriving its spiritual basis from the major religions of the world, Caodaism accepts almost all other faiths and embraces the great prophets along with celebrities from the world of the arts, politics, literature and learning. **The Temple of Literature** in Hanoi, dedicated to the cult of Confucius, is of great historic interest. It is also the scene of water puppet shows.

The former French School of Far-Eastern Studies makes a grand setting for the History Museum.

Quan Thanh (Spirit of the North) Pagoda, on its eastern shore, was erected during the Ly dynasty (1010–1225) and embellished in the 17th century by the addition of a beautiful bell and a 3.4-m-high (11-ft) bronze statue representing the Spirit.

Just across Duong Thanh Nien, the lovers' lane of Hanoi, the West Lake (Ho Tay) is said to have been created by a dragon-king who flooded the entire region in an attempt to drown a wicked nine-tailed fox. Overlooking the lake—an old branch of the Red River—is the 6th-century Tran Quoc Pagoda, one of the most ancient in Vietnam. It has an interior courtyard and a garden containing monastic funerary monuments.

History Museum

Southeast of the old town, between Hoan Kiem lake and the Red River, you will see many noteworthy buildings in typical European architectural style, including the National Library and the Municipal Theatre, built in 1919 and closely resembling the Paris Opera House. Nearby, the History Museum covers all periods from neolithic times to the French colonial era, and boasts fine archaeological exhibits. The dominant theme, however, is the 21 millennia-long struggle against the Chinese.

The Museum of the Revolution is just one block north.

Hai Ba Trung

Among Hanoi's many sanctuaries, the Temple of the Trung Sisters, a 20-minute walk south of Hoan Kiem lake, illustrates the exploits of these two heroines. In the year 40, they bravely drove away the Chinese invaders and were crowned as queens. Three years later, they threw themselves into the river to escape the enemy who had returned in force. An engraved stele recounts their struggle.

Excursions from Hanoi

Within a radius of 100 to 150 km (60–95 miles) from Hanoi, some of Vietnam's most beautiful natural and cultural sites are worth thorough exploration. If you are determined and have a little time to spare, you will discover forgotten historic cities and delightful villages inhabited by ethnic minorities of great charm. These excursions will take you into the breathtaking limestone mountains, where any number of pagodas house welcoming Buddhist communities amid the paddy fields or in caves.

All of these places are accessible in a day trip from Hanoi, provided you set out at sunrise.

An added benefit to starting out in the cool of the morning is that on the way you can watch people going about their daily work: villagers leading their ducks to ponds covered in lotus flowers; fishermen casting their wide nets into the canals; water-buffalo hauling rickety carts through the serene landscape.

Chua Huong

Some places deserve more than a simple day trip, and one such is the Perfume Pagoda, a Buddhist place of pilgrimage in the mountains, 60 km (37 miles) south of Hanoi in the heart of Ha Tay Province. You can make the trip in one day, but three days are hardly enough to do justice to this site. Chua Huong is, in fact, an enormous complex of sanctuaries dotted throughout the forests of a limestone mountain chain.

The road goes as far as the village of Ben Duc, beyond which the journey proceeds by flat-bottomed sampan. This is a magical hour of gliding silently along a labyrinth of canals, encountering the canoes of market gardeners, and floating past mysterious temples. The site itself has a network of steep mountain footpaths linking the twelve principal sanctuaries of the Perfume Pagoda, for the most part built in the 17th century on the mountainside or inside deep caves.

These sacred places, forming two groups of five and seven pagodas respectively, offer wonderful opportunities to the rambler. It would take several days to visit every one of these sanctuaries, an exercise reserved for passionate enthusiasts of Buddhist art. Most people are happy to settle for the glorious ascent up the paved path to Chua Huong Tich, the most interesting of the sacred caves at the summit of Huong Tich, the mountain of the Perfumed Imprint.

Near the landing-stage, there are two temples packed with enough statues and ancient objects to console anyone who feels unable to tackle the long climb up to Chua Huong Tich.

Chua Thay

Dozens of other interesting pagodas are scattered over the countryside surrounding Hanoi. To the west, 40 km (25 miles) from Hanoi, Chua Thay (Pagoda of the Master) in Sai Son village is dedicated to Sakyamuni (Tich Ca) and his 18 *arhats*, or disciples. The villagers also refer to it as Thien Phuc, the Pagoda of Celestial Felicity. The statue of Master Tu Dao Hanh, a skilful water puppeteer of the 12th century, stands next to the statue of his reincarnation, King Ly Thanh Tong.

Tay Phuong

The ironwood Pagoda of the West, 10 km (6 miles) from Chua

SONG HONG, THE RED RIVER

Song Hong, the Red River, has its source in China near Dali, the ancient city of Yunnan. Vietnam's lifeline, 1,149 km (714 miles) long, is one of five fingers of water in the angular peninsula that constitutes South-East Asia. The other four—from east to west—are the Mekong, the Chao Phraya (or Menam), the Salween and the Ayeyarwady. The Red River's waters link the ethnic minorities of the mountainous "blue lands" to the wide plains of the pagoda-dotted "brown lands".

Vietnamese identity was forged in its delta, where the precious silt fertilizes paddy fields and provides clay for the temple bricks—hence providing nourishment for body and soul. The idyllic landscape and smiling people of the delta region radiate a perfect serenity, but don't be mistaken—under the surface roils all the faith and powerful will of Vietnam.

It is not easy to harness this versatile river, whose headwaters are so jealously guarded by China, but the Song Hong, despite its devastating floods, is the true catalyst of Vietnamese unity.

23

A lazy river trip into the verdant landscape of Hoa Lu.

Thay, boasts particularly attractive roofs and 74 statues of *arhats* dating from the 18th century and carved in jack-tree wood.

But Thap

In Ha Bac Province, 30 km (19 miles) northeast of Hanoi, the Pagoda of the Paintbrush, surrounded by a stone gallery, is among the most handsome in Vietnam. It was built in the 12th century but has been remodelled several times since then, acquiring its unusual four-storey octagonal stone *stupa* in the 17th century. Note the ornamental pond carved from rock, next to a delightful stone bridge.

Inside the principal sanctuary, surrounded by a gallery of carved stones, a wooden statue of the goddess of mercy, Quan Am, is here depicted with a thousand arms. There are many other statues, and a fine 13th-century carved wooden prayer-wheel in perfect working order.

Hoa Binh

At the foot of the mountains 80 km (50 miles) southwest of Hanoi, the town of Hoa Binh makes a convenient centre for visiting some of the varied ethnic groups who live in the area: Hmong, Tai, Dao and Muong. The Da river which flows through

24

the town has been dammed just a short distance upstream, creating a reservoir 160 km (100 miles) long. Excursion craft make day trips to tribal villages dotted along its shores.

Hoa Lu

The capital of the Dinh dynasty at the end of the 10th century and that of the Earlier Le at the beginning of the 11th, Hoa Lu is 100 km (62 miles) south of Hanoi and 12 km (7 miles) from Ninh Binh. The ruined citadel is not particularly interesting, but the temples dedicated to Dinh Tien Hoang (11th century) and General Le Hoan (12th century) are worth a closer look.

Many other sanctuaries are scattered throughout this region known as the "dry-land Bay of Ha Long". In fact, with its paddy fields and softly rounded limestone mountains, it more closely resembles the River Li in China, between Guilin and Yangshuo. Boat trips take you into the heart of this natural paradise, where beautiful grottoes shelter a further profusion of temples of great historic and religious significance.

From Hanoi to Ha Long

The best route from Hanoi to Ha Long Bay is the so-called "ferry road", which crosses several branches of the Red River by bridge and causeway.

Haiphong

This route to the bay takes you inevitably to Haiphong, the setting for some of Somerset Maugham's short stories. The second port and third city of Vietnam after Ho Chi Minh City and Hanoi, Haiphong does not have many tourist sights, as it is largely a commercial and industrial city. But if you have some time to spare, do go and see the communal house (dinh) of Hang Kenh, which contains some 500 wooden carvings.

Do Son

About 20 km (12 miles) southeast of Haiphong, the sandy beaches of Do Son, a peninsula with a scattering of islets in a pleasant tropical setting, attract crowds from Hanoi and Haiphong. It's all rather scruffy, including the casino, built in 1994 for foreigners with money to burn.

Cat Ba

The big island of Cat Ba rears up out of the sea only 24 km (15 miles) east of Haiphong. Cat Ba Town, at the western tip, is a busy fishing port as well as a magnet for trippers from the mainland cities. The eastern half of the island is a National Park, much of it forested, with many rare plants. There are few tracks, and not well marked, so trekkers may do well to accept the services of a guide as well as taking plenty of water and insect repellent. The less energetic will be happy to join the local crowd on one of the many boats that make trips in southern Ha Long Bay.

The "Ferry Road"

The 50 km (31 miles) separating Haiphong from Ha Long are totally enchanting, even though the picturesque old ferries have been replaced by modern bridges and causeways. You cross the Red River right in the centre of Haiphong. On the far bank, you plunge into a different world: almost without transition, the trappings of industry give way to a verdant landscape of paddy fields. Bicycles and porters, heavily laden with fruit, vegetables and poultry, enliven the roads. This bustling population owes its economic life entirely to the sea and the cultivated fields.

The huge limestone rocks of Ha Long Bay appear at the end of the road, where they are reflected in the waters of the rice fields. Peasants and water-buffalo alike paddle in the mud, setting the stage for the vista which opens out to the sea at Bai Chay.

Bai Chay

In only a few years this ancient fishing village has evolved into a full-blown tourist resort. It could hardly be otherwise: vast Ha Long Bay, one of the loveliest places in the world by any standards, lies at its doorstep, sprinkled with more than 3,000 small islands whose sheer cliffs rise high up from the sea. Boat excursions take you round this gigantic sculpture gallery. The name of Bai Chay (Scorched Beach) is gradually disappearing from road maps in favour of the more commercial Ha Long Bay City.

Ha Long Bay

To absorb all the magic of Ha Long, you have to spend at least two nights in Bai Chay or Hon Gai, a ferry ride across the next inlet to the east. Leave the port an hour before dawn to see the sun rise over the bay in a dazzling display of gold and purple. It takes a good day to sail around the most beautiful of the natural formations of the archipelago. The cruise ends at twilight, when the limestone rocks of Ha Long catch fire in the setting sun.

Islands and Caves

The classic cruise takes in the Island of Marvels and its cave Hang Dau Go (Wooden Stakes), three chambers festooned with stalagmites and stalactites; Bo Nau (Pelican Cave); Trinh Nu (The Virgin's Cave); Dong Hang Hanh tunnel; the island of Bo Han (Surprise); the Pierced Rock and, last but not least, Ho Ba

Fishing boats enhance the scenic splendours of Ha Long Bay, the eighth wonder of the world.

Hang (the Three Caverns) with its circle of sugar loaf hills, its caves and craggy cliffs—considered the single most spectacular site of Ha Long.

The shores of Hon Gai (Sharp Peak), close to the market and the fishing harbour, provide some equally fine panoramas of the bay. Hon Gai is only a few minutes away from Bai Chay by ferry. The fishermen and market traders crowding around the stalls add a lively human interest.

The North

Living along the Chinese and Laotian borders, Vietnam's ethnic minorities form a world of their own. Most of these peoples, pushed southwards by the Han colonization, fled China centuries ago and headed for the "land of contrary roads".

The 54 Vietnamese minorities are a puzzle for ethnologists. The domain of these peoples who know no frontiers stretches into China, Laos and Cambodia, spilling over into Thailand and Myanmar. Even the best Vietnamese guides, enthusiastic and knowledgeable about cultural matters, are not always able to recognize the races with precision. The only way to distinguish them in some cases is by certain details of their clothing. A good number of these 27 communities have managed to preserve their language and traditions intact.

The ethnic majority of the plains, the Kinh (the Vietnamese proper), who introduced the techniques of rice production and land irrigation, appear to have cultural connections with these mountain-dwelling minorities. They share certain religious beliefs, and there are similarities in their language.

Access to the mountain villages is fairly easy provided you are ready to forego the usual comforts of the traditional hotel. Bamboo channels supply water for domestic purposes and for irrigating the paddy fields. Travellers in a hurry can still en-counter some of these minority tribes in small groups at the markets of Lang Son and Cao Bang, or along the tarred roads leading to these two cities. But it's worth recalling that here, and indeed anywhere with access to motor vehicles or television, the "Vietnamization" of these colourful ethnic people is inexorably taking place.

Lang Son

Set in a landscape of paddy fields only 18 km (11 miles) from the Chinese border, over 200 km (124 miles) north of Hanoi, Lang Son was sacked by Chinese troops during their brief 1979 incursion. Encountering stiff resistance, the Chinese alone counted

THE MEO ZAO

The sixth-largest ethnic minority of China with almost 6 million members (recorded as the Miao people in the census), the Meo Zao (or Dao) were driven out of their homeland in central Asia at the time of the great Han expansion. They are now found, with their cousins the Yao (1.5 million in China), scattered thinly throughout the whole of South-East Asia. They are slowly abandoning their slash-and-burn cultivation methods for more conventional agriculture, an evolution that is leading them toward a more sedentary lifestyle.

The Meo Zao are a minority people with rather sophisticated traditions. The various communities share a common origin but do not necessarily resemble each other. However, one feature they do share is their painstaking concern over beautifying themselves. The women adorn themselves with a king's ransom in silver jewellery, but some of their customs are less attractive to Western eyes—the Vietnamese Zao, for example, protect their teeth with a spectacular coat of black lacquer.

more than 20,000 dead. The town lies at a strategic point on the road and railway leading to Guangxi Province. The frontier was reopened in 1992 to foreigners wishing to see both countries during the same holiday; however, you will need a visa. Cross-border trade is booming, and Ky Lua market is full of Chinese imports as well as local produce and ethnic clothing and crafts.

Apart from the market, the main place of interest in Lang Son is the Tam Thanh pagoda, set in one of a number of grottoes near the town.

Cao Bang

There is little of interest in this other frontier town, but the mountains, grottoes, lakes and waterfalls of Ba Be national park, inhabited by the Dai and Zao peoples, are sufficient reason to make an expedition (by four-wheel drive vehicle) into the countryside. You can view the abundant bird life, take boat trips on Vietnam's largest natural lake and visit its islands. The park's guest houses offer simple accommodation.

Hang Pac Bo

On the border with China, two hours' drive from Cao Bang, Pac Bo cave, in a rugged mountainside, was briefly the home of Ho Chi Minh when he entered Vietnam in 1941 to organize resistance against the French. He named the nearby river Lenin and a mountain Karl Marx. A few memorabilia have been installed in the newly built Ho Chi Minh Museum.

Sa Pa

Another place where you can encounter ethnic tribes is the hill station of Sa Pa, founded in 1918 by French colonists. At an altitude of 1,600 m (5,250 ft), it lies at the foot of Fan Si Pan, the country's highest peak at 3,143 m (10,312 ft).

Three trains per day link Hanoi with the Chinese frontier. The railway line follows the Red River, cutting through spectacular landscapes and ending at the border town of Lao Cai. From there, you can wind your way by bus or taxi through the countryside to Sa Pa some 30 km (19 miles) distant. The Hmong, Zao and Yao people who inhabit this region are very friendly, and it is easy to mingle with them at the Saturday market. Walkers will enjoy the steep 9-km (5-mile) hike to the top of Fan Si Pan.

Dien Bien Phu

From Sa Pa to Dien Bien Phu it's a hard day's drive on twisting roads; some travellers prefer to break the journey with a night's stop at Lai Chau, a sleepy former provincial capital. An alternative to the road journey is the rapid air shuttle that flies several times a week between Hanoi and Dien Bien Phu, but then you will miss out on the principal attractions of the trip, which are the ethnic minorities and the changing countryside along the roadside. Along the valley slopes you'll see the stilt houses of Thai farmers; the Hmong live higher in the hills.

However, many enthusiasts of military history come to Dien Bien Phu to see for themselves the battleground where the French war in Indochina was finally lost. It was here that the French Army, completely surrounded by the forces of the Vietminh, was obliged to surrender on May 7, 1954 after a siege that lasted 57 days. Fifteen thousand French soldiers had been posted to this valley to deny the Vietnamese troops access to Laos. In December 1953, 50,000 men of the Vietminh, commanded by General Vo Nguyen Giap, began their encircling movement. The attack on Dien Bien Phu was launched on March 13, 1954. To the surprise of the French, the Vietnamese were equipped with artillery and subjected the defenders to a ceaseless bombardment. The final number of casualties may never be known. More than 3,000 French soldiers were killed and many were wounded, while the Vietnamese losses are estimated at more than 20,000.

You can appreciate the scale and significance of the siege and Vietnamese victory at the Museum of the Armies and the memorial erected in 1984 to commemorate the victims who lie beneath the paddy fields.

3

THE THREE LOVELIEST LANDSCAPES The region of rice paddies and limestone promontories near the citadel of **Hoa Lu** composes a superb backdrop similar to that of Ha Long Bay; it is equalled only by the tableau of green fields and sugar-loaf mountains around Ben Duc, along the canals leading to the **Perfume Pagoda**. But Vietnam is a kaleidoscope of magnificent landscapes, and for our third choice, it's a toss-up between the seascapes of the **Hué coast at Nha Trang**, the light of the **Mekong delta** near Can Tho, and the **terraced hillsides** of the mountain-dwelling ethnic minorities.

The Mandarin Road

History has endowed Vietnam with a spine in the shape of the Mandarin Road linking North to South and, in particular, Hanoi to Ho Chi Minh City. Renamed Colonial Road No. 1 by the French, and now simply National Road No. 1, it was the historic "express" route of the Mandarins from China to the Mekong delta. A vital thoroughfare paralleled by a railway line, the Mandarin Road today provides a condensed panorama of the country's numerous attractions.

Thanh Hoa

Between Hanoi and Hué, the road passes through Ninh Binh, in the region described on p. 25.

North of Thanh Hoa, the strategic bridge of Ham Rong, carrying both the road and the railway line, was bombed on several occasions between 1965 and 1972 by the US Air Force.

At the nearby village of Dong Son, jewellery, bronze drums and other objects from one of Asia's oldest civilizations have been discovered. These treasures are on display in museums in Hanoi, Ho Chi Minh City—and as far away as Paris.

Thanh Hoa, a quiet little town some 60 km (37 miles) south of Ninh Binh, is a centre for excursions to see the fishermen on stilts and the fine sandy beaches of Sam Son 15 km (9 miles) to the southeast.

Lam Son

Le Loi, who repulsed the Chinese in 1427, was born in Lam Son, 50 km (30 miles) northwest of Thanh Hoa. Here you'll see remains of the citadel of Lam Kinh, tombs of the Le rulers and the temple housing the bronze statue of Le Loi. A stele proclaiming his victory over the Ming dynasty stands at the edge of the lake. The Ho dynasty citadel is in the neighbouring village of Tay Giai.

South to Vinh

Road No. 1 south of Thanh Hoa, as far as the outskirts of Hué, is littered with historic sites and traces of the Vietnam War, each with its baggage of tragic or glorious memories of bombardment, napalm attacks, massacres and death. Nature is slowly recovering its former beauty. The mountains of Annam sweep down to the sea, and the road winds through stately forests and offers 31 fine sea views. Local inhabitants produce attractive pottery and raise silkworms.

Vinh, the provincial capital, is of little interest—the region is one of the poorest in the country—except for its role as birthplace of many men of letters and revolutionaries. But only 20 km (12 miles) away is the fishing village of Cua Lo, where you can sample local seafood and see how *nuoc mam*, the famous salty fish sauce, is made—and enjoy its magnificent white sands.

Kim Lien

If you are keen to see some Ho Chi Minh memorabilia, you can, like the Vietnamese pilgrims, make the 15-km (9-mile) detour west of Vinh to the valley of the Lam River and the village of Kim Lien, his birthplace. Ho's house, now a museum, stands in a garden near a lotus pond.

Hoang Son

South of Ha Tinh, the Hoang Son mountain chain stretches from Laos to the sea. This natural barrier at about 1,000 m (3,300 ft) above sea-level, is crossed by way of the Deo Ngang pass. It separates Tonkin from Annam, the "Dominion of the South" which the Vietnamese took from the Cham people in the latter part of the 10th century. This rugged frontier, which once separated the empires of China and India, today simply divides the provinces of Ha Tinh and Quang Binh.

Phong Nha

Close to the village of Bo Trach and 25 km (15 miles) from Dong Hoi, a fishing port and capital of Quang Binh Province, the grotto of Phong Nha is hidden in a landscape of conical hills. It comprises several caverns bristling with stalactites and stalagmites; the longest is visited by boat. Remains of Cham altars and inscriptions underline the grotto's use as Buddhist sanctuaries in the 9th and 10th centuries. Upstream, divers have discovered a vast network of tunnels and caves.

The Demilitarized Zone

From 1954 to 1975, the Ben Hai River was the frontier between North and South Vietnam, separated by a Demilitarized Zone, or DMZ. For Vietnam veterans and other political and military strategy buffs, this has become a place of pilgrimage. The Hien Luong Bridge, 178 m (584 ft) long, links both parts of the reunified country.

The national cemetery of Truong Son, dominated by a monument on the crest of a hill, aligns endless rows of gravestones, representing some of the 300,000 soldiers of Vietnamese origin declared missing in action.

A symbol of resistance, the underground village of Vinh Moc was pounded systematically by American bombers. Labouring in horrifying conditions, 24 hours per day for 18 months, resistance fighters tunnelled out a network of passages—in some places 10 m (33 ft) below the surface—as a storehouse for arms and provisions destined to supply their forces in the South. You can visit the narrow tunnels, but don't venture inside if you suffer from claustrophobia. Nearby, in startling contrast, you can relax and swim at the splendid palm-fringed beaches.

Ho Chi Minh Trail

When the Americans established the McNamara Line, an impenetrable electronic curtain, the North Vietnamese opened the Ho Chi Minh Trail through the Annamite Cordillera and Laos. They transported weapons, munitions and provisions along it to their allies in the South. Tens of thousands of soldiers died in this huge sector along Road No. 9 and scattered with military bases: Doc Mieu, Con Thien, Camp Carroll and chiefly Khe Sanh (now marked on maps as Huong Hoa). Thousands of US marines were stationed here, with a mission to disrupt movement through the DMZ and along the Ho Chi Minh Trail. In 1968, North Vietnamese

forces surrounded and attacked Khe Sanh, in a prelude to the Tet offensive. Massive aerial bombing just saved the Americans, who later pulled out to avoid their own version of Dien Bien Phu.

Hué

Ancient Phu Xuan, the splendid Imperial City of Hué, embraces the most fascinating historical sites in Vietnam. The capital of Annam is endowed with handsome old buildings and romantic countryside all around.

Built on the banks of Huong Giang, the Perfume River, on an ancient Cham settlement, Hué reflects the power and magnificence of the Nguyen dynasty of emperors and empresses. Its architecture is harmoniously integrated into the landscape, though some of the buildings—modelled on Chinese constructions of the Qing dynasty (1644–1911) show a surprising lack of audacity. With its river valley ringed by five mountains (representing the five elements), the location of Hué is said to conform perfectly to the rules of cosmology.

Devastated and pillaged on countless occasions, notably by the French in 1885 and during the Tet offensive in 1968, the Imperial City has nevertheless retained some remarkable monuments. Its palaces and pavilions bear witness to its past grandeur. At one

time or another, it has welcomed the nation's greatest intellectuals and artists—poets, painters and musicians. The active restoration campaign led by UNESCO is bringing back some measure of its earlier lustre.

Hué cooking is a special treat: restaurants and food stalls serve the local specialities—crisp pancakes, spicy noodles and tasty snacks wrapped in banana leaves.

The Citadel

Start your visit at the citadel, protected by 10 km (6 miles) of ramparts and a moat 40 m (130 ft) wide. Built between 1804 and 1832, its three enclosures symbolize three sources of power. Kinh Thanh, the Capital City, was the domain of the mandarin hierarchy. Hoang Thanh, the Imperial City, was an intermediate space where grand official ceremonies and audiences were held. Tu Cam Thanh, the Forbidden Purple City, was the private sector reserved for the emperor and the imperial family, and had the finest buildings. However, it was sacked and razed to the ground, and apart from the Royal Theatre and the Library, which have been restored, only ruins remain.

The Gate of Humanity, one of ten entrances in the walls of the Imperial City.

Wars, floods, fires and termites have all taken their toll. The temples, palaces and monuments which miraculously still stand bear witness to the magnificence of Hué at the beginning of the 19th century, when the Nguyen emperors held sway over a unified Vietnam.

Several objects which survived the Vietnam War are displayed in the Imperial Museum within the citadel.

The Imperial City

Pass through the outer wall by way of the Ngan Gate, with the tall brick Flag Tower (Cot Co) to the left. Ahead is the massive Ngo Mon (Noon Gate) which gives access to the Imperial City. Two stairways lead up to the Belvedere of the Five Phoenixes on top of the gate, a grandstand for the emperor to watch various ceremonies unfolding below.

At the centre of a great courtyard of frangipani trees, the shimmering effects of the Golden Waters Pool set off to perfection the Cau Trung Dao, a bridge reserved exclusively for the emperor. Stone tablets on the Great Greetings Esplanade (Dai Trieu Nghi) mark the places allotted to the mandarins who came to offer greetings to him, traditionally seated on his royal throne in the Palace of Supreme Harmony (Dien Thai Hoa). Lavishly deco- 35 rated and carved, the palace occupies 1,400 sq m (15,000 sq ft) and presents a harmonious ensemble after its skilful restoration by UNESCO.

Temples

Several interesting temples have withstood the ravages of time and war and celebrate the various Nguyen cults.

In the southwest corner of the Imperial City, The Mieu (Temple of Generations), with ten decorated altars, is dedicated to the ghosts of almost all the departed rulers of the dynasty. Facing it are nine masterpieces of 19th-century bronze, the dynastic urns (Cuu Dinh) 2 m (6 ft) high, weighing 1,900 to 2,500 kg (1.9 to 2.5 tons) and symbolizing the might of the Nguyen emperors. Each one, supported by three legs, is richly ornamented with animals and country scenes in relief. Immediately behind them is a handsome three-storey pavilion.

Pagodas

Hué is a city as sacred as it is historic, with over a hundred Buddhist temples and shrines. Many are worth seeking out, such as Tu Dam Pagoda, famous throughout the land; it was founded by a Chinese bonze, or Buddhist priest, at the end of the 17th century.

Another interesting excursion takes you to Thien Mu, the Pagoda of the Celestial Old Lady, 4 km (2 miles) from the citadel (an easy bicycle ride). Now the most venerated shrine in all Vietnam, it was built by Lord Nguyen Hoang in 1601, in response to the apparition of an old woman. She predicted to the local inhabitants that a prince would arrive and erect a temple of supernatural significance on the site, in order to ensure the prosperity of the country.

Look for an enormous bronze bell weighing over 3 tons, cast in 1710, and a marble tortoise, the symbol of longevity, bearing a stele carved with the story of the rise of Buddhism in Hué.

The seven-storey octagonal tower of Happiness and Grace (Phuoc Duyen) was added in 1840 by Emperor Thieu Tri. Each storey represents a different reincarnation of Buddha; originally there was a statue of the deity on every floor. Climb to the top for magnificent views over the Perfume River from a height of 21 m (69 ft).

The Imperial Tombs

In the luxuriant setting of the Hué hills, south of the Perfume River, the splendour of the imperial tombs compensates for the destruction suffered by the citadel. Amid fields of manioc and sugar cane, rice paddies and forest, the seven tombs (lang tam) of 19th and 20th-century Nguyen emperors, complete with statues and stelae, could almost be considered an oriental counterpart to Egypt's Valley of the Kings.

At the Tu Duc mausoleum, 7 km (4 miles) from Hué, Chinese gardens with lotus-filled ponds and shade-giving giant banyans complement the monumental gates, courtyards, palaces and pavilions, all linked by grand stairways and sculpture-filled terraces. The mausoleum is built along two parallel axes, one for the tomb and one for the palace. An avenue leads to a lotus pond with a fishing pavilion on stilts. From there, follow the path to the Salutation Courtyard, with two rows of mandarins and traditional animal sculptures, opening on to the octagonal Stele Pavilion containing a stone inscribed with praises of the emperor. Beyond this is a crescent-shaped lake, and finally the elaborately decorated tomb itself, guarded from evil spirits by a protective wall.

A stony gaze at Khai Dinh's tomb, the last mausoleum of the Nguyen dynasty.

The second path from the pond takes you to the emperor's palaces and pavilions, which he occupied in his lifetime with 104 wives and concubines. The prodigious number of his companions was of little value for posterity, however, as he produced no male heirs.

To the south is the tomb of Thieu Tri, similar to that of his father, Minh Mang (see below), but smaller and more discreet, according to his wish for something economical and convenient.

The reinforced concrete mausoleum of Khai Dinh, to the southeast, was built in the 1920s and its architecture may take you aback. Many find it rather kitsch, contrasting too sharply with the peaceful mountain setting. The Honour Courtyard contains a profusion of stone statues of mandarins, horses and elephants. The tomb and shrine of Khai Dinh, at the top of some stairs, has a gilded bronze statue of the emperor on his throne, holding a jade sceptre. These all stand apart from the murals and floors composed of gaudy mosaics made of glass and porcelain fragments.

In the middle of a pine forest, the Minh Mang Mausoleum, 12 km (7 miles) from Hué, can be reached by boat along the Perfume River. It is built on a single axis, flanked by two great lakes and outylying pavilions. An esplanade decorated with stone statues links the Salutation Courtyard, the Stele Pavilion and various other temples and pavilions. Beyond it, a second esplanade crosses the Lake of Pure Limpidity by way of three small bridges, leading to three terraces and the emperor's pavilion of eternal rest.

The tomb of the first Ngyuen emperor, Gia Long, is the furthest from Hué, 16 km (10 miles) to the south. Surrounded by mountain peaks and shaded by pine trees, the complex also contains the tombs of members of the imperial family.

Lang Co

Continuing south along the Mandarin Road, you'll come to the oyster-fishing village of Lang Co, 68 km (42 miles) from Hué on a spit of sand between the sea and the lagoon. Its long palm-fringed beaches and the delicious seafood will tempt you to stay for a while. The road then climbs to a new 6.2-km tunnel which enables you to bypass Hai Van, the Pass of the Ocean Clouds, at 496 m (1,627 ft), and save up to an hour on journey time. At Lang Co, an old French fort, occupied in turn by the Americans and the Vietcong, has better withstood warfare and defoliants than the surrounding forest. In the 15th century, the Hai Van pass marked the frontier between Vietnam and the kingdom of Champa.

Danang

In the centre of the country, Danang is one of Vietnam's biggest cities, a major port and the focus of huge expansion and development, with new beach resorts planned. One of its main attractions is the Cham Museum.

Bao Tang Cham Museum

Entirely devoted to the enigmatic Cham civilization, the museum was built in 1915 by the French School of Far-Eastern Studies. More than 300 rare objects have miraculously survived to testify to the high degree of culture of Champa, the Hindu kingdom which occupied the centre of Vietnam down as far as the Mekong—and most notably the Danang region—after the end of the

2nd century. Among the greatest treasures of the 9th and 10th centuries, when Cham art was at its peak, are several sandstone sculptures representing the Hindu deities Garuda, Ganesh, Brahma, Vishnu and Shiva, a bevy of seductive dancers, *lingas* (phalluses) and hemispherical breasts representing the mother-goddess.

The Marble Mountains

The most popular excursion from Danang is to the Marble Mountains 10 km (6 miles) south, where hills represent the five elements: Kim Son for metal; Thuy Son water; Moc Son wood; Hoa Son fire; Tho Son earth. The highest outcrop, Thuy Son, rises 106 m (348 ft) and is pierced with grottoes *(dong)* where the Hindu altars of the Cham have been replaced by Buddhist shrines. Huyen Khong is the most spectacular cave, measuring 35 m (115 ft) from floor to ceiling. It served as a refuge for Vietnamese soldiers during the war. Four stone spirits watch over this sacred historic site consecrated to the Buddhist, Confucian and Brahman religions. An immense concrete statue of Buddha stands in Hoa Nghiem grotto.

Minh Mang's beautiful mausoleum is a haven of tranquillity.

Hoi An

Large burial jars (up to a metre high) and fragments of pottery from the Sa Huynh period confirm the existence of Hoi An, a small town south of Danang, 2400 years ago. From the 2nd to the 10th centuries, it was the hub of the kingdom of Champa and benefited from the flowering of its culture. The port—formerly known as Faifo—was already open to the world when the Western countries set up their first trading posts here and their ships plied the maritime Silk Route. It supplied European and Oriental merchants with ivory, mother of pearl, medicinal plants, paper, lacquer, cloth, porcelain, pepper and other spices. In the 17th century, when merchant ships from Portugal, France, Holland, Japan and China all traded here, it was one of the most significant ports in South-East Asia. The Japanese and Chinese, then other foreign colonies, set up shop, the European settlers often accompanied by missionaries. But by the 19th century the port had silted up, and Danang took over its role.

UNESCO has recorded more than 850 monuments of historic interest in Hoi An: wells, bridges, houses, shops, temples, pagodas and tombs. The assembly halls and houses *(hoi quan)* that the Chinese community built here at the beginning of the 19th century are still the model for Chinese dwellings in Vietnam today. All told, Hoi An offers an exceptional architectural primer, and the constant renovation of its historic buildings has maintained it as a living museum in excellent condition. The best way to see all its treasures is to hire a guide.

Japanese Covered Bridge

Despite the attractions of the houses in the old town, the premier site remains Cau Nhat Ban, a covered bridge built by the Japanese community in 1593 to link its quarter to that of the Chinese. There are statues of two dogs at one end and two monkeys at the other; some say the bridge was begun in the year of the monkey and completed in the year of the dog, while others claim the animals represent points of the compass. A small pagoda (Chua Cau) was built on the north side of the bridge to protect sailors.

Several traditional houses in the area, such as Tan Ky and Diep Dong Nguyen, display a combined Japanese and Chinese influence, as do several communal houses of the Chinese congregation.

By the Thu Bon River, near the sampans, modern Vietnamese life revolves around the colourful and lively marketplace. If you have a few hours in hand you can have a shirt made to measure.

My Son

A mere 30 km (19 miles) separate Hoi An from My Son, the spiritual city of the Champa kingdom from the 4th to the 12th centuries, and the burial place of many of its rulers. The area fringing the road between the two towns is scattered with isolated Cham sites. Tra Kieu, previously Simhapura, affords glimpses of the ruins of its ancient ramparts; the 9th-century tower-temple of Bang An, the only known octagonal Cham building, has been restored more or less successfully; and the ruins of Dong Duong, a Mahayana Buddhist monastery built at the same time on the site of Indra-

pura, the capital of Champa between 860 and 986, reminds us that at this time the kingdom was partially converted to Buddhism.

Sheltered in a circle of hills, My Son was dedicated to the Hindu deity Shiva. Of its original 68 impressive brick monuments, only 25 are still standing. Having withstood half a millennium of exposure to the elements, they were destroyed in just a few years by American bombing and ground-fighting between the US forces and the Vietcong. There is nothing left of the main tower, reduced to dust in 1969, and despite recent restoration, the jungle has not yet been cleared from all

CHAMPA

The people of the kingdom of Champa were of Indonesian origin and spoke a Malayo-Polynesian language, but they became Indianized towards the end of the 2nd century AD through trade with that great Hindu culture, reaching a high level of civilization. Their talents were multi-faceted: the seafarers dominated the silk and spice trades, the agricultural specialists produced a fast-growing variety of rice which revolutionized China in the 13th century, and constructors developed hard-wearing brick-building techniques.

King Bhadravarman created the religious centre of My Son in the 15th century, and his successors never stopped embellishing it. The kingdom was feared and respected, but the advent of a new and ambitious Vietnam to the north in the 15th century was destined to transform the country's frontiers. The Great March South of the Vietnamese, the Nam Tien, dismantled the kingdom of Champa in 1471 after taking the capital, Vijaya. The few hundred thousand Cham of South-East Asia today are dispersed among the ethnic minorities of that vast region, but within Vietnam's borders there are still some to be encountered in Ninh Thuan Province near Phan Rang.

Nha Trang has retained much of its old-fashioned charm.

of the site. There remain a few sculptures and bas-reliefs of Shiva, Parvati and Nandi, a temple to Bhadreshvara and a library with floral decorations, but it requires a great deal of imagination to conjure up the beauty of My Son at its peak. The best surviving vestiges can be seen in the Champa museum at Danang.

Inland Route

Instead of following the coast south of Danang, you can head into the Central Highlands, by road or (if short of time) by air. The main towns, Kontum, Pleiku (or Play Ku) and Buon Ma Thuot, are not the chief attractions; they were the scene of heavy fighting in the Vietnam war and have been rebuilt in functional style. Visitors are drawn instead by the chance to meet some fascinating minority groups, by the scenery and the wildlife.

Minority Groups

People of the Bahnar hill tribe live in tall, thatched stilt houses near Kontum; some have been adapted to host groups of trekkers for dinner and overnight stays. Around Pleiku are scattered the villages of the Jarai, such as Plei Boum—another place where visitors are accommodated in stilt houses.

Yok Don National Park

Some 40 km (25 miles) northwest of Buon Ma Thuot, the park includes dry forest typical of South-East Asia, the home of tigers, 200 species of birds, variegated monkeys and elephants, wild and tamed. At Ban Don village, near the entrance to the park, you can meet the Ede people, known as skilled elephant trappers and tamers. Some of them still live in extended family groups of up to 40 in traditional longhouses.

Nha Trang

From My Son to Nha Trang, the Mandarin Road passes several Cham temples, but it is the coastline beyond Qui Nhon which is chiefly of interest along this route. For 230 km (143 miles) until it reaches Nha Trang, the road passes fishing villages alternating with emerald lagoons, empty beaches and secret inlets. After the wide Van Phong Bay you will see the white hills of the salt pans at Ninh Hoa, an opportunity to take some fantastic photographs before you arrive at Nha Trang, the friendly capital of Khan Hoa Province.

Nha Trang enjoys a privileged situation beside a natural harbour. Its 8-km (5-mile) beach of fine sand is dotted with numerous hotels, from colonial era to modern, to suit every budget and with every comfort, from swimming pools and fine restaurants to shows and nightlife. In fact, Nha Trang is the biggest seaside resort in the whole of Vietnam, and most water sports are available here. In addition, there are several places of cultural or historic interest close to the town centre, and excursions are organized to outlying islands.

The Harbour

The day begins at 5 a.m. with the arrival in the port of the fishing boats, inevitably accompanied by a great commotion as fishermen cry their wares and stalls are quickly set up on the quayside.

You can also explore the boatyards, where large wooden fishing boats are still being built.

Beaches

On the town beach, it's difficult to avoid the attentions of swarms of hawkers selling soft drinks and souvenirs. If you are looking for solitude, nowhere can beat the deserted inlets and virgin strands along the Mandarin Road.

Yersin Museum

At the colonnaded Pasteur Institute, south of the Post Office by the waterfront, a museum is dedicated to the biologist Alexandre Yersin (1863–1943), where you can see his desk and library. Of mixed French and Swiss parentage, Dr Yersin was born in Au-

43

bonne on Lake Geneva, Switzerland, and came to Vietnam in 1889 after having worked with Louis Pasteur in Paris. Six years later, in Hong Kong, he discovered the bubonic plague bacterium (now called *Yersinia* in his honour), and shortly afterwards founded the Pasteur Institute of Nha Trang. Yersin introduced the hevea (rubber tree) and the cinchona (the tree from which quinine is extracted) into Indochina.

Long Son Pagoda

Decorated with dragon mosaics made from shards of glass and pottery, the Long Son pagoda, on the west side of town, recalls the tomb of Khai Dinh at Hué. The sanctuary was built in 1963 in front of a hill topped with an enormous white Buddha seated on a lotus flower. Memorials honour the monks and nuns who committed self-immolation in protest against the repressive Diem regime.

Po Nagar

Built between the 7th and 12th centuries, the "Lady of the City" is better preserved than most of Vietnam's Cham sites, despite severe erosion. There's no need to fight your way through jungle to see it—you just have to climb to the top of a hill overlooking the harbour and the fishing port, to the north of town.

Of the ten towers that formed the sanctuary of Kauthara in the southern Cham empire centuries ago, four still guard the town of Nha Trang and its rivers. The 14 columns of a *mandapa*, or meditation room, stand in front of the acropolis. The great North Tower, Thap Chinh, covered by a tapering pyramidal three-storey roof, is a fine example of Cham architecture. Over the entrance to this *kalan* is a four-armed dancing Shiva with one foot resting on the head of the bull Nandi, and inside is the goddess Po Ino Nagar, a female form of Shiva. The tower was built in 817 to replace the temples destroyed 43 years earlier by Malay pirates intent on stealing a golden linga. Another gold linga, set in place in 918, was stolen by the Khmer. This persuaded Jaya Indravarman I to replace it by a black stone statue representing the ten-armed Goddess Uma, thus removing further temptation.

Hon Chong

A short walk north of Po Nagar, the promontory of Hon Chong (Husband Rocks), 4 km (2.5 miles) from the town centre, overlooks the clear waters of the South China Sea, with views of the coastal mountains and nearby islands, in particular Hon Do (Red Island) which is crowned by a Buddhist temple.

Buzzing with noise and colour, Nha Trang's little fishing harbour.

Cau Da

At the southern end of Nha Trang's beach, beyond the principal hotels, the villas of Emperor Bao Dai have been converted into a luxury hotel set in a large park. It crowns the top of a hill, enjoying lovely views of the bay and its fishing village. The Institute of Oceanography and Aquarium, built in 1922 at the Nha Trang end of the village, has tanks of rays, seahorses, lobsters, turtles and other marine fauna.

Island Cruises

The most memorable excursions from Nha Trang call at the islands just off the coast for diving,

snorkelling, a visit to a restaurant or just a relaxing day out. There is no lack of choice, as there are 74 islands in the Province of Khanh Hoa alone.

The most popular island, easily accessible and practically crawling with seafood, is Mieu, where you can visit picturesque fishing villages and a gigantic fishery in the open sea. Choose your own fish and seafood from among the 50 varieties on offer, and take your "catch" to one of the small restaurants on stilts along the shore. When the cruise returns at noon, you will find your tuna, lobster, crayfish, crab, and so on, deliciously grilled and seasoned. 45

Monkey Island (Dao Khi), as its name implies, is inhabited by these appealing creatures. Bamboo Island (Hon Tre) and Ebony Island (Hon Mun) are popular with divers and snorkellers.

If you are fond of bird's-nest soup, you will probably be interested in seeing the two Swallow Islands (Hon Yen) where a limited number of licensed "hunters" are authorized to go twice a year to collect the precious nests, made from the solidified salivary secretions of the swallow.

Cham Temples

Between Nha Trang and Ho Chi Minh City (Saigon), the Mandarin Road passes through several pretty coastal stretches.

Cam Ranh Bay was a huge US naval base in the Vietnam war, and was later used by the Soviets before the fall of the USSR and the departure of the Russians.

Further south, you will notice the silhouettes of Cham temples beside Road No. 1.

Po Klong Garai

From Phan Rang-Thap Cham, 103 km (64 miles) from Nha Trang, turn west onto the Dalat road (No. 20) to reach one of the finest monumental Cham groups, 6 km (4 miles) inland.

Po Klong Garai stands on the crest of a sandstone hill visible from the road. Outlined against the sky, four 13th-century towers on a vast brick esplanade make a striking architectural statement. The *kalan* (sanctuary) is decorated with a multitude of statues, some occupying all the niches on the façade and others emerging like bristling gargoyles from every angle of the roof. A carved, six-armed Shiva is carved above the entrance, with inscriptions all around the door-frames.

4

THE FOUR MOST INTERESTING CHAM SITES

The ancient Hindu kingdom of Champa once occupied the centre of Vietnam, a region which has inherited some traces of this civilization. Its four most beautiful sites are to be found in the jungle of **My Son**, its spiritual capital; at the sanctuary of **Po Nagar**, on a hill overlooking Nha Trang; near Phan Rang-Thap Cham on the Dalat road at the summit of the Cham Acropolis of **Po Klong Garai**; and further south on another hill at **Po Rome**. The finest sculptures discovered at these sites are on display at the Cham Museum in Danang.

Beyond the vestibule and its traditional white statue of the bull Nandi, an unusual *mukha-lingam* appears beneath a wooden vault, surrounded with offerings and sticks of incense. This stylized phallus symbolizes the virility and creative force of Shiva, and bears, presumably as a gesture of reverence, a painted face thought to be a likeness of King Po Klong Garai, who reigned from 1151 to 1205.

Po Rome

One of the last sanctuaries of Cham civilization, Po Rome (or Ro Me) lies 15 km (9 miles) south of Phan Rang-Thap Cham, on high ground at the end of a 6-km (4-mile) track to the west of Road No. 1. This region is inhabited by large communities of the minority Cham, and you will see many families along the track, which is passable only in dry weather. You will have to park your vehicle and walk for about 10 minutes to reach the hill on which the 16th-century Cham temple stands. Stairways lead to the top.

The entrance is surmounted by a six-armed dancing Shiva. Inside the temple, the usual symbols of agricultural fertility, two stone statues of white Nandi bulls, stand guard before an altar. Above it is a magnificent bas-relief dedicated to King Po Rome, one of the last Cham rulers (1625–51), deified in the form of Shiva. He died a prisoner of the Vietnamese.

Dalat

The winding scenic mountain road heading inland to Dalat passes through some beautiful countryside. At an altitude of 1,300–1,500 m (4,260– 4,920 ft), Dalat is the capital of Lam Dong Province, where the perpetual spring-like climate offers a different aspect of Vietnam. The hill station owes its reputation to Dr Yersin (see p. 43), who discovered the cool, healthy site in 1893. The Valley of Love and its lake, busy with small boats, the legendary Lake of Sighs, the Summer Palace of Bao Dai, the last emperor, and a number of colonial villas still draw Europeans as they did in the early 20th century, and you will find all the hotel facilities you could wish for.

Town Centre

Dalat has expanded in a rash of ugly concrete buildings, including the large Central Market, a popular meeting place for the ethnic groups from the high plateaux that run from the centre of the country to the western border. There is usually a colourful and photogenic array of exotic fruit and vegetables.

47

Emperor Bao Dai's golf course on the shores of Xuan Huong lake has been renovated. At the northeast end of the lake, the Flower Garden displays roses, camellias, liles and other tropical plants, and there's an orchid house.

The cathedral, south of the market, has colourful stained-glass windows made in France. it was built from 1931 to 1942.

East of town the Railway Station is popular with railway enthusiasts. It has a coal and oil-burning steam engine, and there are twice-daily excursions to a nearby village in a Russian-built diesel car.

Pagodas

North of Dalat, the Thien Vuong Pagoda, built in the 1950s, has three gold-lacquered sandalwood statues, 4 m (13 ft) high, each weighing almost a ton and a half.

South of town, the Linh Son Pagoda (1842), reserved for men only, has an enormous bronze and gold bell and is fronted by two dragon balustrades.

Around Dalat

In the nearby villages you can meet the many tribes of mountain dwellers living in wooden stilt-houses. These include the Lat, Koho, Chill, Ma, and Maug peoples. If you continue northwards to the plateaux of the neighbour-ing Dac Lac Province, you will encounter other ethnic minorities—and elephants.

Waterfall Road

The journey along Road No. 20 passes through magnificent country with some of the most breathtaking waterfalls in the land.

The Prenn Falls, 16 m (52 ft) high, are only 13 km (8 miles) from Dalat and make a very popular outing for the Vietnamese. More spectacular, the Lien Khuong Falls, 36 km (22 miles) from Dalat, tumble through virgin forest, where the River Da Nhim cascades over a cliff 18 m (59 ft) high.

The Gougah Falls are a little further on, about 40 km (25 miles) from Dalat. Follow a track to the left off Road No. 20 and after a 10-minute walk the splendid sight of this natural wonder will come into view, parted at the centre like a curtain by a huge volcanic rock.

The watery spectacle continues with the Pongour Falls, 54 km (33 miles), from Dalat and then a further 8 km (5 miles), along a small road. You can also see the Bo Bia Cascade 6 km (4 miles) from Di Linh among the tea plantations, and lastly the Dambri Falls, possibly the highest in the country at 90 m (295 ft). The water plunges into a sink-hole surrounded by tropical vegeta-

An interesting choice for your picnic, displayed on a sea-front stall.

tion. Access is from Bao Loc by an easy road, 16 km (10 miles) through plantations of tea and mulberries.

To reach Ho Chi Minh City, the road crosses Lake La Nga on a mighty bridge which affords views of picturesque lake houses on stilts, built by fishermen who have settled on this artificial lake abounding in underwater life.

Phan Thiet

The Mandarin Road swings away from the coast before meeting it again at the major fishing port of Phan Thiet, where the quayside market generates an entertaining pandemonium every morning.

East of the town is a long arc of south-facing sandy beaches, stretching for most of the 22 km (14 miles) to Cae Mui Ne. Near the cape itself the sands turn red and rear up in spectacular dunes. Inevitably, developers were attracted to this piece of shoreline, which looks set to rival Nha Trang as Vietnam's top resort, especially as it's quite accessible from Ho Chi Minh City. A number of hotels have sprung up, with facilities for a full range of water sports. They have become a favourite with tour groups, both for beach holidays and for overnight stops on the way north or south.

49

Vietnam's premier port, Ho Chi Minh City (HCMC), former Saigon, is also the largest city in the land. Official figures put the population at 5 million, but if you include its sprawling suburbs, this busy capital boiling with life actually numbers 7 million inhabitants.

Ho Chi Minh City

While HCMC is of limited interest to anyone in search of the exotic, Vietnam "old hands", French and American alike, must surely feel some nostalgia when revisiting the modern city, packed with bittersweet memories. Graham Greene's fictional "Quiet American" would have trodden these streets during the US–Vietnam War.

City Centre

The twin spires of the red-brick neo-Romanesque Notre Dame cathedral, built between 1877 and 1880, rise 40 m (131 ft) over a grassy square in the middle of the commercial centre and embassy district. The Central Post Office, designed by Gustave Eiffel, also looks onto the square.

South along Le Duan avenue, Reunification Hall, formerly the Presidential Palace, is a concrete replacement built after rebellious South Vietnamese pilots bombed the old one in 1962.

Nearby is the War Crimes Museum, with helicopters, tanks and bombs in the courtyard. Military atrocities are analysed in graphic and disturbing detail, photographs and exhibits illustrate the inhumanity of mankind.

East of the cathedral is the Revolution Museum. From here you can walk south to the Ben Thanh covered market and the Hindu temple, Chua Ba Mariamman, said to be the scene of several miracles. The guardians Maduraiveeran and Pechiamman stand beside the goddess Mariamman, preceded by two lingas. The temple's towers are encrusted with intricate decorations.

Leading east from the cathedral, Duong Dong avenue is lined with hotels and restaurants all the way to the Saigon River. The Municipal Theatre, built at the beginning of the 20th century, is also in this area, along with art galleries, souvenir shops, the large stores and the mosque. Floating restaurants are to be found in this quarter, moored at Bach Dang Quay close to Me Linh Square, presided over by a statue of General Tran Hung Dao, 51 conqueror of the Mongols. The Saigon River, which links the city to the sea with 117 km (73 miles) of waterway, is open to craft of all kinds. However, the floating restaurants only venture as far as the port on their gastronomic and musical cruises.

If you follow Le Duan avenue northwards from the cathedral, you will first reach the Military Museum, then the Botanical Gardens and Zoo. The History Museum, within the grounds, houses the famous bronze drums from Dong Son and many sculptures and other artefacts from Oc-Eo, the archaeological site of the ancient kingdom of Funan. More of these sculptures are on view in the Art Museum on Pho Duc Chinh Street, south of the centre, which also contains some beautiful Cham sculpture. There are many antique shops in this area, and an army surplus market.

Pagodas

North of the centre, in the Da Cao district beyond La Van Tam Park, the Pagoda of the Jade Emperor (Phuoc Hai Tu) was built in 1909. Its different rooms contain a multitude of large papier-mâché statues of warriors, generals and divinities, all drowning in incense fumes. The Taoist Jade Emperor Ngoc Hoang, wrapped in shining red garments, is in the middle of the principal sanctuary, surrounded by his four guardians, the Great Diamonds, whose gaze is as glittery as the gem they are named after. In a small chamber, twelve ceramic statues of female figures represent the twelve months of the Chinese calendar and symbolize the chief features, good and bad, of the human character.

The Giac Lam (Forest of Enlightenment) Pagoda, 8 km (5 miles) west of the centre, was

5

THE FIVE MOST APPEALING PAGODAS The strangest is the **Perfume Pagoda**, a group of 12 sanctuaries set in the magnificent limestone mountains of Ha Tay Province, south of Hanoi. In the east, the **Paintbrush Pagoda** bristles with handsome carved stone monuments. In Hanoi, the pretty **One Pillar Pagoda**, shaped like a lotus, recalls a charming legend. The **Celestial Old Lady Pagoda** in Hué boasts a three-ton bronze bell and a marble tortoise. In Ho Chi Minh City, the **Giac Lam Pagoda** is a fine example of Vietnamese architecture.

built in 1744 in typical Vietnamese style and most recently renovated in 1900. As well as its Bodhi tree, it houses many original statues of Buddha, several gilded. Notice the unusual Tree of Wandering Souls, formed out of 49 lamps and statuettes of Buddha. Four times a day (4 and 11 a.m., and 4 and 7 p.m.), prayer ceremonies accompanied by singing, gongs, bells and drums bring a bit of life to this tranquil temple.

The architecture of the Giac Vien (Buddha's Complete Enlightenment) Pagoda, southwest of Giac Lam, has much the same features, down to identical statuary such as the laughing Ameda beckoning little children to him.

Cholon

The Chinatown of Cholon is an integral part of HCMC, and despite the authorities' anti-Chinese campaign of 1978–79, the population of this huge and dynamic quarter, the Hoa, still speak Cantonese or Mandarin and dialects derived from it.

The town is completely dedicated to commerce—its name means "Great Market"—and there are bazaars all over the place. Not only will you find all Western products, but also, and at lower prices, a profusion of useful and practical goods (medical equipment, Swiss army knives with the white Swiss cross replaced by the Vietnamese star, cigarette lighters, spare parts for bicycles and cars, etc.), and a host of items artfully manufactured or salvaged from the detritus of our consumer society, such as old tin cans, worn tyres and military equipment left behind by the American army.

There are numerous temples here in Chinatown, and several of them are well worth a look: Thien Hau for its painted ceramic sculptures; Phuoc An Hoi Quan for its porcelain miniatures, its sacred objects and the life-size sacred horse of Quan Cong. Ong Bon boasts a carved wooden altar; Phung Son has countless statues; Tam Son Hoi Quan is richly decorated. Khanh Van Nam Vien is known for its exemplary Taoism; Ha Chuong Hoi Quan for its frescos and the stone pillars carved in China. Last but not least, Quan Am is renowned for the gilded statue of A Pho, the Queen of Heaven, and its roof decorated with ceramics.

The Catholic Church of Cha Tam was the last refuge of President Ngo Dinh Diem before his execution in November 1963. Cholon's market, Binh Tay, overflows everywhere onto the street with fruit, vegetables, fish and meat. These complete the list of principal attractions in Vietnam's liveliest city.

53

Excursions from Ho Chi Minh City

It's worth devoting a whole day to Tay Ninh and the tunnels of Cu Chi, northwest of Ho Chi Minh City. If you're longing for a beach, head for Vung Tau or, even better, Long Hai.

Tay Ninh

The Holy See of the Cao Dai religion, the third-largest in the country after Buddhism and Catholicism, is at Tay Ninh, 100 km (62 miles) northwest of HCMC. This small town, whose inhabitants are mostly Vietnamese with Khmer and Cham minorities, has given its name to the province, which juts into Cambodia.

Founded at the beginning of the 20th century in the village of Long Hoa near Tay Ninh, Caodaism has its spiritual sources in an amalgamation of the best aspects of the great ancient religions of the world, Buddhism, Christianity, Confucianism, Taoism, Hinduism and Islam, coloured by Spiritualism and a touch of opportunism. Caodaism is the prime example of religious syncretism. This openness to all philosophies helps to avoid any forms of fundamentalism.

The Great Temple

In the entrance hall of the Great Temple, a fresco depicts the signatories of the "Third Alliance between God and Man", the three Caodaist saints: Nguyen Binh Khiem (1492–1587), an Annamite poet and man of letters; Victor Hugo (1802–85) in the robes of a member of the French Academy; and Sun Yatsen (1866–1925), the revolutionary and founder of the Republic of China. The alliance ecumenically unites Jesus Christ, Buddha, Mohammed, Confucius, Joan of Arc, Shakespeare, Pasteur, Lenin, Churchill, Descartes and the astronomer Flammarion!

The rococo extravaganza of this holy city, dominated by the Great Temple, takes its inspiration from every architectural style imaginable. Beyond the immense nave, supported by pillars carved with dragons, is the Globe of the Most High, a monumental blue sphere scattered with stars and the "Divine Eye"—the most venerated emblem of Caodaism, symbolizing God.

Above the altar are the six key personages of Caodaoism: Sakayamuni, founder of Buddhism; Ly Thai Bach, a fairy of Chinese mythology; Khuong Tu Nha, the Chinese saint Jiang Taigon; Lao Tse, the founder of Taoism; Quan Cong, the Chinese god of war (Guangong); and Quan Am, the Chinese goddess of mercy (Guanyin). Ceremonies take place four times a day, every six hours. The principal service starts at noon, when the excursion groups from HCMC have delivered their busloads to fill the galleries. Cardinals, priests, deacons and other male and female dignitaries, in mandarin-style robes, enter in procession along the great nave. They are grouped according to the colour of their robes, with men on one side and women on the other. In the upper gallery, a choir sings hymns, accompanied by an orchestra. Now and then, women in the centre of the nave sing and beat wooden drums.

With its dazzling cathedral-pagoda and the choreography of participants in bright robes, the Holy See of Tay Ninh is an undeniable tourist attraction. A pilgrimage here can be rounded off by a trip to the beautiful surrounding countryside planted with rubber trees and to the tunnels of Cu Chi.

Cu Chi

Used by the Vietminh and Vietcong in their wars against the French and Americans, the tunnels of Cu Chi are 50 km (31 miles) from Ho Chi Minh City on the Tay Ninh road, and tour operators usually bring their flocks here as part of an excursion to the Caodaist Holy See. However, they are mainly of interest to war

The ornate cathedral of the Cao Dai religion in Tay Ninh.

veterans and students of guerilla warfare, and are not the most uplifting attractions of Vietnam.

The complex of 350 km (217 miles) of tunnels on three levels was excavated between 1948 and 1973. After a walk through the stuffy, extremely narrow corridors, where you can peer into chambers fitted out as kitchens, dormitories, shelters, hospitals and conference rooms, you tour a small part of the densely booby-trapped 420 sq km (162 sq miles) of terrain described as the "most devastated, bombarded, defoliated and gassed in the whole history of warfare".

Vung Tau

Only its proximity to Ho Chi Minh City 120 km (75 miles) away accounts for the reputation of Vung Tau, formerly the French beach retreat of Cap St-Jacques, as a seaside resort. Its beaches, cliffs and temples are not without their attractions, but the nearby construction of the vast international port of Sao Mai and the exploitation of rich offshore deposits of oil and gas could well wipe out any holiday-geared expansion.

The very beautiful beach at Long Hai, 40 km (25 miles) away on the Ho Chi Minh City road, is better suited to Western taste and would seem to have a brighter future.

The Mekong Delta

Land and water meet and mingle where the great Mekong river splits into nine main channels and countless creeks. To the south and west of Ho Chi Minh City, this vast, flat landscape makes up 10 per cent of the country's area but produces almost 40 per cent of the rice crop, and much else besides. This intensive agriculture is a relatively recent development; not until the French colonial period was the effort of taming the floods and tides thought to be worthwhile. A road journey through the Delta is continually interrupted by the need to wait for a ferry, but there's so much to see that a delay is no penance. Better still is to take a boat trip, to see the floating markets and the amazing variety of craft and cargoes.

Virtually inaccessible, the marshiest areas and mud flats covered at high tide are a paradise for wading birds. Closest to the sea, thick curtains of mangroves border vast expanses of water where the silence is disturbed only by the shrieks of birds and the slither of crocodiles. The humid horizons of the Mekong delta provide an astonishing variety of landscapes, but however idyllic, they remain at the mercy of thoughtless human exploitation, pollution and hydrological disturbance.

My Tho

Ideal for a one-day excursion from Ho Chi Minh City for those who would like at least a brief look at the Mekong, the city of My Tho is mainly of interest for the activity on its river and its colourful market. However, organized excursions include a mandatory stop at the Vinh Trang Pagoda, the snake farm at Dong Tam, and a boat trip on the Mekong to the Island of Phung, known as "The Island of the Coconut Monk" because of a hermit who spent a contemplative life there existing on nothing but coconuts.

But there's no need to emulate him, as the Mekong delta is abundant in other fruit. The sampans that cross the various tributaries, especially at Vinh Long and Can Tho, carry melons, bananas and durians to the markets, contributing to the general hustle and bustle of life on the river.

From Vinh Long, admirers of the French writer Marguerite Duras's books make a pilgrimage

THE MEKONG

The third-longest river in Asia (4,220 km, or 2,620 miles), the Mekong rises in the highlands of Tibet and empties into the sea at the extreme south of Vietnam, having irrigated the Chinese provinces of Szechwan and Yunnan, and Myanmar, Laos, Thailand and Cambodia along the way. The Vietnamese call it Song Cuu Long, the Nine Dragons River, these being the nine branches of the famous delta, the rice bowl of the country. The last region to be conquered and annexed by Vietnam, the delta belonged to the Khmer kingdom until the 18th century.

The river reaches its highest level in September. Like the Red River, its continual deposit of silt extends the shoreline 70 to 100 m (230 to 330 ft) into the South China Sea each year. The land is so low-lying that the twice-daily tides can reach as far as 300 km (186 miles) inland. By a curious natural phenomenon, the immense Cambodian lake Tonle Sap, which empties into the Mekong at Phnom Penh, sees the course of the river reverse during periods of flooding, which allows it to hold back enough water to prevent dramatic inundation in the delta region. However, the deforestation of Cambodia is imperilling this ecological balance. An increase in the salt water flowing in from the sea could have serious consequences for the fertility of the land. As well as rice, the Mekong delta produces many fruits and vegetables, notably sugar cane and coconuts.

to Sa Dec, to see the famous house of the Chinaman featured in *The Lover*.

Can Tho

At the heart of an important network of canals and rivers, Can Tho is the best base for excursions around the delta. The hotel infrastructure is excellent, the floating market at Cai Rang (half an hour by boat) is alone worth the journey—as is that at Phung Hiep—and the roads and waterways together offer rapid access to all the attractions of the Mekong.

Into Cambodia

In one or two days, starting at Can Tho, it is possible to make the journey northwest as far as the Cambodian border, passing through Long Xuyen and Chau Doc, where many Cham, Khmer and Chinese live; each community has its own temple. Mount Sam, 5 km (3 miles) southwest of Chau Doc, is no more than a hill, but it rises steeply from the rice paddies and offers good views of the Delta and into Cambodia. The hillside is scattered with pagodas, grottoes and assorted tourist "attractions" intended to appeal to the many local visitors. They flock especially to the gaudy Tay An Pagoda near the foot of the hill, filled with colourful statuary. From Chau Doc, it's possible to

take a river boat to the Cambodian capital, Phnom Penh.

Birdwatching

Another one- or two-day circuit will appeal mainly to bird spotters. Taking you to the south, it includes Soc Trang (Khmer Museum and the Bat Pagoda), Bac Lieu (bird sanctuary and Khmer Pagoda), and Ca Mau, hidden away in the mangrove forest of U Minh. Ca Mau is interesting for the Ngoc Hien ornithological nature reserve, but take note that its marshes are mosquito-infested.

To the Gulf of Thailand

Another unusual trip goes first to Rach Gia, northwest of Can Tho. The port, with its agricultural and fish market, its pagodas and its Caodaist temple, is home to large numbers of Khmer and Chinese. In the dry season, it is possible to visit the site of the ancient city of Oc-Eo. The principal artefacts unearthed are on display in the History Museum and Fine Arts Museum in Ho Chi Minh City.

The excursion continues as far as Ha Tien, on the Gulf of Thailand. The coastline is wonderful, with unspoilt beaches stretching as far as the Hon Chong Peninsula, caves transformed into temples, and small islands like the heavenly Nghe or the hilly Phu Quoc.

Shopping

The opening of the country to foreign tourists has given local artisans a new lease of life. The tradition of one street, one commodity is continued here with modern products such as electronics and safes. This is a good place to get new prescription spectacles, delivered the day after an eye test at very low cost.

Antiques

The export of antiques is regulated and requires an export licence. Vietnamese items are more difficult to find, the market being dominated by Thai, Burmese and Chinese examples. If you are looking for a bargain, you need to be a connoisseur as fakes are common. As an alternative, the museums usually have a shop selling reproductions of the originals on display in their galleries.

Ceramics and Fabrics

Pottery, porcelain and ceramics with designs in cobalt blue on a white background are widely available in every shape and size, from ashtrays to coffee services. It may be more difficult to find a suitable place in your living room for the imposing multicoloured elephants or statuettes of Buddhist divinities. You may prefer the magnificent embroidery in shimmering colours that brightens up sheets, pillowcases and tablecloths.

Tailors can produce made-to-measure suits and dresses in 48 hours. The ladies' *ao-dai* can be made to order, though it is also available more cheaply off the peg. This garment will tempt anyone with an eye for a striking design. It consists of a knee-length tunic slit down both sides and is usually worn over wide trousers. A versatile outfit, the *ao-dai* needs only a conical hat to set it off to perfection.

Lacquerware and Silk-screen Painting

The arts of lacquering and painting on silk are two areas in which Vietnamese craftsmen excel. Both techniques originated in neighbouring China, and are carried on today in time-honoured fashion.

Genuine lacquer is the sap of the tree *Rhus vernicifera*, native to the Far East, which is extracted and left to oxidize and harden in the open air. This results in a liquid as thick as syrup. It was 59

Vietnam's markets are picturesque, varied and colourful.

initially used as a protective varnish for wood. The basic lacquer colours of red, black and brown are combined with paint of other shades to enrich the overall effect. A coat of lacquer is applied over each layer of colour: the most beautiful antique items can have up to two hundred layers. Lacquered objects of all kinds are to be found in the souvenir shops, sometimes inlaid with fragments of duck-egg shell. Bargaining is expected, except in the state-run stores.

The favourite subjects for silk painting are scenes from daily life in the villages and fields, perhaps with a pagoda or a view of Ha Long Bay in the background. Pastel shades depict the changing colours of the seasons, with the texture of the silk lending a hint of romanticism. Glued to a paper backing, the pictures are easy to transport flat at the bottom of a suitcase.

Yet More Souvenirs

Chinese carpets, prints, engravings, leather goods, wooden carvings, green tea and spices are bound to satisfy the most ardent shopaholic. Collectors will probably like to browse among old stamps, coins, medals and colonial helmets (very often brand-new "aged" copies).

Dining Out

Like other South-East Asian cuisines, many Vietnamese dishes are variations on the great Chinese gastronomic tradition. The similarity ends when it comes to the way certain ingredients are used. Vietnamese cuisine is spicier than southern Chinese, and contains great quantities of green vegetables and aromatic herbs. Rapid cooking—in broth, by steaming or by stir-frying— is the sacred technique used to prepare the 500 or so recipes making up the Vietnamese cookbook.

Nuoc mam

The true national seasoning of Vietnam, *nuoc mam*, or fish sauce, plays the same role as traditional Chinese soy sauce. It is produced by packing fish into jars between layers of salt and letting it all ferment. The brine which results turns out to be quite nutritious. Diluted with water or lemon juice, and enhanced with chilli or sugar (when it is called *nuoc cham*), *nuoc mam* is served with every meal, either separately as a seasoning or added during cooking. After the initial surprise, the palate soon becomes accustomed to the flavour which is so fundamental to Vietnamese cuisine.

Rice and bread

Vietnam is both a major consumer of rice and a major producer (fifth on a world scale). The fertile deltas of the Mekong and the Red River produce two or three rice harvests per year, composed of four different varieties. The staple of the daily diet, rice is served at every meal. It is also the main ingredient of transparent thread noodles and of the delicious *nems*.

A legacy of colonial days, the French *baguette* is to be found in every marketplace and on every restaurant table.

Soups and snacks

Pho, which originated in the North, is a soup of transparent thread noodles enriched with beef or chicken and flavoured with nuoc mam, ginger, coriander and other spices. This popular dish is served at all hours of the day from pavement restaurants (beware however of the general level of hygiene!). The equivalent in 61 the South is *hu tieu*, a soup of pork or crab and shrimp.

Another traditional dish is *goi*, a term encompassing various salads and raw vegetables (not for delicate stomachs!) topped with thinly sliced meat and garnished with coconut, peanuts and fried onion.

Familiar specialities in many Chinese and Vietnamese restaurants in the West, *nem* (in the north) or *cha gio* (south) are universal favourites. A small, delicate spring roll, the *nem* consists of a fine rice pancake wrapped around a tasty filling of crab, pork, thread noodles, onions and mushrooms. They are deep-fried and served on a bed of salad, to be enjoyed with the indispensable *nuoc mam* and fresh mint leaves.

Meat and Fish
Stock-rearing is uncommon in Vietnam. Beef *(bo)* and lamb are expensive. On the other hand, pork *(lon)* figures more frequently on menus, along with chicken *(ga)* or duck *(vit)*. The rivers and streams produce an abundance of freshwater fish and crustaceans, and the South China Sea delivers up a fresh harvest daily: shrimp *(tom)*, crab *(cua)*, shellfish and fish of all sorts. Among the many specialities is the Hanoi favourite *cha ca*, fish grilled with aromatic herbs and accompanied by noodles and peanuts.

Desserts
Rice is often one of the ingredients used in the preparation of sweet dishes such as *banh com*, where a portion of rice is stuffed with bean paste and coconut. Another such dish is *banh deo*, a cake of rice flour, sesame seeds and candied fruits. Baked custards *(che)* are widespread, prepared with soya cheese, maize, coconut milk and lotus seeds.

Drinks
Green tea is the national drink. Good, light, local beer *(bia)* is available everywhere, and you could always try the rice wine. Mineral water *(nuoc suoi)* should never be drunk except from a sealed bottle. The fresh fruit juices are a delicious way to quench your thirst, but do not add ice cubes, which may have been made from contaminated water.

A Basic Culinary Vocabulary

bread	*banh mi*
coconut milk	*nuoc dua*
coffee	*ca phe*
fish	*ca*
fruit	*trai cay*
meat	*thit*
milk	*sua*
noodles	*bun*
rice	*com*
salt/pepper	*muoi/tieu*
stir-fried vegetables	*rau xao*
sugar	*duong*
tea	*nuoc tra*

Sport and Entertainment

With 3,260 km (2,000 miles) of coastline, Vietnam is perfect for water sports, practised mainly around the areas of Ha Tien, Vung Tau and Nha Trang. Golf is developing slowly, although it is still considered a rich man's game. Night-owls can experiment with karaoke or check out the local discothèques.

Ball Games

Left to grow wild after the departure of the French, the country's golf courses are now being revived. Green fees can be extortionate, but they are gradually coming into line. There are courses at Ho Chi Minh City, Vung Tau, Dalat and Hanoi. The Vietnamese are great enthusiasts of football and tennis, and also excel at badminton, volleyball and table tennis.

Water Sports

Dazzled by the cultural riches of the country and exhausted by sightseeing, you may fancy a few days of rest and relaxation by the sea. You'll not be disappointed, as many resorts can match the Mediterranean. Tourist development is in full swing, but some of the most beautiful beaches are not yet equipped with facilities. Such is the pace of change, however, that things may have improved by tomorrow.

The popular resorts of Ha Tien, near the Cambodian border, and Vung Tau, near Ho Chi Minh City, tend to get very busy at weekends. At present, though, Nha Trang is the best-equipped and the "in" place for diving and snorkelling. Surfing and wind-surfing are slowly gaining in popularity.

Other Activities

Nightlife in Vietnamese cities is very much the same as you'd find anywhere in the world. There are cinemas, theatres, discothèques and nightclubs in all the large cities, and karaoke bars are all the rage.

Gambling is once more permitted: the Vietnamese enjoy a legal flutter at the races, on slot machines and in lotteries; and illegal betting at dominos, mah-jong and cock-fighting is just as popular. Several casinos have been opened, some of them reserved for foreigners.

63

The Hard Facts

Here are some the practical details you will need to know when planning your trip to Vietnam.

Airports

Tan Son Nhat international airport is 7 km (4 miles) northwest of Ho Chi Minh City.

Noi Bai international airport is 45 km (28 miles) north of Hanoi.

Both airports handle several flights per day from Europe, mainly via Bangkok, Kuala Lumpur, Hong Kong and Singapore. They both have money-changing facilities.

Buses and taxis are available for transport to the city centres.

Climate

The climate is not uniform from north to south, so the weather is always good somewhere in Vietnam. The best months are from October to April.

From December to February it can be cool and rainy in the north, average 13°C (55°F) but warm in the south, average 24°C (75°F). The monsoon affects everywhere except the centre from May to September, with temperatures reaching 35°C (95°F) in the south, and bright intervals between the downpours. Along the coast of the central region, the months of September to January are the wettest.

Communications

Post your letters in Hanoi or Ho Chi Minh City, from where they will take about 10 days to arrive in Europe. Fax messages can be sent from the principal postal centres.

Outgoing international telephone calls are made through the operator. There are telephone boxes which take cards, but calls abroad remain expensive. At the post office, there is a minimum charge of three minutes. In the hotels, rates are astronomical.

The dialling code for calls to Vietnam is 84. The city code for Hanoi is 4, for Ho Chi Minh City, 8.

Internet cafés have sprung up in the cities and some smaller towns. Charges are very reasonable. The business centres of some international hotels also allow e-mail access.

Currency

The Vietnamese unit of currency is the New Dong (D).

Banknotes are issued in denominations from 100 to 100,000 *dong*. Coins are obsolete, except for collectors. The rate against the US dollar is nowadays very stable: a hundred or so dollars will make you a *dong* millionaire. Buy dollars before you leave home and take a substantial stock of small denominations. They can be exchanged for *dong* in any bank or currency exchange office. Payment in dollars is welcomed everywhere, as long as the notes are in good condition.

Credit cards are accepted by some banks, the luxury hotels, the airlines and the large official travel agencies, but they charge a commission. Only travellers cheques in US$ can be converted into dollars or *dong*; other travellers cheques such as sterling can be changed into *dong* only.

Customs

You are allowed to bring into the country 400 cigarettes or 50 cigars or 100 g tobacco; two bottles of alcoholic beverages and a reasonable quantity of perfume.

There is no limit to the import of foreign currency but amounts exceeding US$3,000 in cash must be declared on arrival. You can export up to the same amount, but proof of expenses is required. The import and export of local currency *(dong)* is prohibited.

Electricity

In all the hotels, the supply is 220 volts AC, 50 Hz, though a few, rare places still have 110 volts. Plugs are European-type, with two round pins. Power cuts are frequent in the south in the dry season (January to May).

Embassies and Consulates

Your embassy or consulate will be of help if you get into serious trouble, if you lose your passport, for example. Most countries are represented in Hanoi and Ho Chi Minh City.

Emergencies

Police 113
Fire 114
Ambulance 115

Entry Formalities

Visas are required. A passport valid for at least one month after your return is necessary in order to obtain a visa. If you are travelling with a tour operator, they will take care of all the formalities on your behalf. Allow a month for the documents to be prepared.

An important point: make several photocopies of your passport, including visa, and keep them in several different places (pockets, suitcase, camera-case, etc.), to avoid having to hand over the original whenever possible, and thus reducing the risk of loss. 65

You can also scan them and send them as an attachment in an e-mail addressed to yourself, so you can retrieve them wherever you are.

Essentials

Light cotton clothing such as shorts, bermudas, skirts and T-shirts are ideal for the south, with jeans and a sweater for the north. A light raincoat will be useful wherever you go. A pair of trainers, sandals and slip-ons for the evening are adequate as footwear. Carry a minimum of clothing as all city hotels have an efficient 24-hour laundry service. You can always buy extra items fairly cheaply on the spot.

A hat, sunglasses, sunblock cream and insect repellent are vital, not forgetting a pocket-lamp for when you visit caves or if there is an electricity cut. Leave some space in your suitcase or take an empty bag for the gifts and souvenirs which you will undoubtedly want to bring back.

Health Precautions

No vaccinations are obligatory, but it is prudent to have valid poliomyelitis and tetanus protection. Vaccination against hepatitis B is strongly recommended. A malaria preventative should also be taken, according to your doctor's or pharmacist's recommendations.

The basic travelling medicine chest should include drugs for intestinal problems, travel sickness and allergic reactions (insect bites).

In recent years, Vietnam has greatly improved its food hygiene standards. Nevertheless, it is only sensible to observe a few basic rules: never eat raw vegetables or fruit that you have not personally peeled. All water should be considered potentially contaminated. Drink and brush your teeth with bottled mineral water (and make sure the seal is intact), boiled or purified water (buy tablets before leaving home). Fresh fruit juice is excellent, but avoid the ice cubes. Milk should also be boiled, or reconstituted from powdered or tinned milk using pure water.

Languages

Vietnamese is the language of the vast majority, but Chinese, both Mandarin and Cantonese, is the second national language, spoken by many of the substantial ethnic Chinese minority.

English is most commonly spoken in the south (partly as a legacy of the American presence, but also reflecting growing trade, tourism and educational influences). A knowledge of French survives among the declining number of old people who experienced the French colonial era. Russian is slowly dying out.

Opening Hours

For rural Vietnamese the working day begins at dawn and ends early in the afternoon.

State-run shops, banks and offices generally open Monday to Friday 8–11 a.m. or noon and 2–4 or 4.30 p.m. Private shops open 8.30 a.m.–7 p.m., those of Ho Chi Minh City sometimes closing later. Street traders stay open as long as there are clients to buy their wares.

Post offices open every day, including holidays, 7 a.m.–8 p.m.

Public Holidays

These are the official public holidays, but there are also many religious festivals specific to each province.

January 1	New Year
End January–beginning February (1st–7th day of the 1st lunar month)	
	Festival of Tet (New Year)
February 3	Creation of the Vietnamese Communist Party
April 30	Reunification (Liberation of Saigon)
May 1	Labour Day
May 19	Birth of Ho Chi Minh
September 2	Proclamation of the Republic in 1945, the National Day
December 25	Christmas Day

Security

Even in the big cities, there is not much crime in Vietnam, nor are there organized gangs. The population is very hospitable and respectful towards foreign guests. Keep an eye open for pickpockets in crowded places. Avoid any display of wealth, and leave your jewellery, money and important documents (passport, airline ticket) in the hotel safe.

Social Customs

The respect of certain rules and customs is, as everywhere else, an elementary rule. In Vietnam, shoes are removed before entering religious sanctuaries and dwellings. In general, women should avoid being too skimpily clad in the temples and forego topless bathing on the beach. Small problems are best resolved with a smile. It is a pointless exercise to show displeasure or impatience. You will be better served by explaining calmly but firmly the reasons for your complaint without losing your sense of humour. Vietnamese are conciliatory and civilized. It is the custom to shake hands when meeting someone.

Time Difference

Vietnam operates at GMT + 7, which means six hours ahead of western Europe in winter and five hours ahead in summer.

Tipping

Service charges in large hotels and restaurants are generally included in the bill. If you stay more than one night in a hotel, you could leave a little extra for the chambermaid. In smaller restaurants and bars, a tip for good service is always appreciated, and baggage porters expect a tip. If you use the services of a driver or a guide, it is normal to give US$3 per day to the driver and US$5 per day to the guide.

Transport

There are regular flights from Hanoi and Ho Chi Minh City to all the principal towns of Vietnam. It is advisable to reserve seats several days in advance. Helicopter flights are organized from Hanoi to Ha Long Bay.

Vietnam has a railway network running principally along the coast from Ho Chi Minh City to Hanoi (a two-day journey!) and Haiphong. But the rates for foreigners are not much cheaper than air fares. For information, see www.vr.com.vn (the web site of Vietnam railways). To call up the English version, look at the end of the three lines of red text beneath the banner.

Buses are incredibly cheap and reach even the most inaccessible parts of the country. Comfort, reliability and safety are in proportion to the price.

Individual travellers may find that a private car with driver is the most practical way of getting around: this way you can stop whenever you wish. Driving yourself can be hair-raising. Traffic drives on the right.

In town, the cycle-rickshaw (cyclo) is by far the best method of transport: agree on the price before you set out. Metered taxis are available in the large cities.

Chua Tran Quoc

Ho Tay

Duong Thanh Nien

Quan Than Pagoda

Ho Truc Bach

Duong Yen Phu

Cau Long Bien

Red River

Pho Thuy Khue

Hoang Hoa Tham Pho

Stadium

Pho Nguyen Truong To

Quan Thanh

Phan Dinh Phung

Botanical Garden Bach Thao

Presidential Palace

Ho Chi Minh Mausoleum

Pho Gam Cau

Duong Tran Nhat Duat

Duong Dieu

Hung

Citadel

Nam De

Pho Hang Khoai

Pho Hang Chieu

Nguyen Sieu

Chua Mot Cot

Stadium

Pho Cua

Nguyen

P. Hang Vai

Museum of Independence

Cau Chuong Duong

Ho Chi Minh Museum

Pho Le Hong Phong

Hoang

Dong

Pho Hang Bo

Pho Hang Bac

Duong Tran

Duong

Flag Tower

Army Museum

Tran

Phu

Ly

Phuong

P. Hang Quat

Pho Hang Gai

P. Cau Go

Den Ngoc Son

Theatre

Museum of Fine Arts

Nguyen

Thai Hoc

Hang Bong

Pagoda

Ho Hoan Kiem

Cultural Palace

Quang Khai

Van Mieu

Pho Ton Duc Thang

Pho

Pho Trang Thi

P. Nha Chung

Park I. Ghandi

National Exhibition

Museum of the Revolution

Duan

Hai

Ly

Ba

Pho Hang Khay

Pho Trang Tien

Museum of History

Le

Pho

Thuong

Tien

Trung

City Theatre

Hanoi Tourism

Museum of Geology

Tran

Kiet

Hung

Dao

Pho Kham Thien

Pho

Nguyen

Vietnam Tourism

Ho Thien Quang

Du

Ba

Hong

Pho Tran Khan

Circus

Tran

Nhan

Tong

Hue

Hom Market

Lo

Tru

N

500 m

Park Lenin

Van Ho Exhibition

Pho

Pho

Pho

Nguyen Cong

Hai Ba Trung Pagoda

Duc

HANOI

Ho Ba Mau

Ho Bay Mau

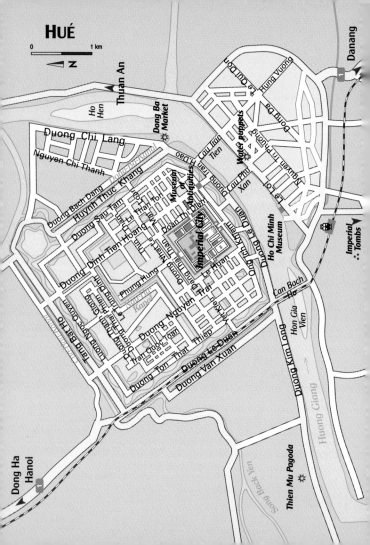

HUÉ

0   1 km

N

Danang

Thuan An

Ho
Hen

Dong Ba
Market

Duong Chi Lang

Nguyen Chi Thanh

Le Qui Don

Hung Vuong

Dong Da

Nguyen Tri Phuong

Duong Bach Dang

Huynh Thuc Khang

Duong Sau Tam

Duong Dinh Tien Hoang

Le Thanh Ton

Museum of Antiquities

Tran H. Dao

Cau Dong Tien

Cau Phu Xan

Water puppets

Le Loi

Doan Thi Diem

Imperial City

Ho Chi Minh Museum

Duong Le Duan

Imperial Tombs

Phung Hung

Xuan Phu Canal

Le Huan

Can Bach Ho

Hon Gia Vien

Duong Dinh Thi Ho

Duong Ngoc Quyen

Duong Nguyen Trai

Le Thi

Tran Quoc Toan

Duong Ton That Thiep

Duong Le Duan

Duong Van Xuan

Duong Kim Long

Huong Giang

Tang Bat Ho

Dong Ha
Hanoi

Song Bach Yen

Thien Mu Pagoda

HO CHI MINH CITY CENTRE

0   500 m

N

Rach Thi Nghe
Rach Phu Thi Nghe

Dai Lo Tran Quang Khai
Tran Hung Dao
Phuoc Hai Tu
Duong Nguyen

Phan Dinh Phung
Sau
Duong Dinh Tien Hoang
Minh Khai

Vinh Nghiem
La Van Tam Park
Dien
Stadium
History Museum

Thang
Chinh
Duong
Thi
Ha Ba Trung
Military Museum
Zoo
Botanical Gardens

Ly
Duong
Nam
Duong
Duong
Le Duan
Ton Duc Thang
Binh Khiem

Railway Station
Phu
Ky Khoi
University
Pasteur
Notre Dame Cathedral
Nguyen
Du
Ly Tu Trong
Don Dat
Dang

Phung Son Cha Tam Giac Lam Pagoda Giac Vien Pagoda
Bien
Dien
War Crimes Museum
Huynh Tan Cong Chua
Reunification Hall
Pasteur
Municipal Theatre
City Hall
Central Mosque
Me Linh Square

Xa Loi
Cach
Chien
Truong
Revolution Museum
Nghia
Dai Lo Nguyen Hue
Old Market
Bach
Ben
Song Sai Gon

Culture House
Mang
Cong Vien Park
Dinh
Chua Ba Mariamman
Ben Thanh Market
Duong
Le
Huynh Thuc Khang
Dai Lo Ham Nghi

Theatre
Thi Xuan
Tam
D. Pham Hong Thai
Ferries to Mekong Delta

Duong
Bui
Trai
D. Le Lai
Lao
Dao
Art Museum
Calmette
Cong Truc
Nguyen
Ho Chi Minh Museum

Nguyen
D. Pham Ngu
Hung
Nguyen Thai
Phung Son Tu Pagoda
Duong
Duong
Tat

University College
Tran
Dinh
Lo
Co Bac
Co Giang
Ho
Don
Nguyen
Truong
Thanh

Dai Lo
Nguyen Van
Xu
Ben
Chuong
Ngu
Rep
Van
Ben

Cholon
Dai Lo Tran Hung Dao
Cu
Kenh
Duong

INDEX

Bai Chay 26
But Thap 24–25
Cambodia 58
Can Tho 58
Cao Bang 29
Cat Ba 25–26
Cau Da 45
Champa 41
Cham temples
    46–47
Cholon 53
Chua Huong 22–23
Chua Thay 23–24
Cu Chi 55–56
Dalat 47–49
Danang 38–39
Demilitarized
    zone 32–33
Dien Bien Phu
    29–30
Do Son 25
Ferry road 26
Gulf of Thailand 58
Ha Long Bay 26–27
Haiphong 25
Hang Pac Bo 29
Hanoi 17–22
Hoa Binh 24–25
Hoa Lu 25
Hoang Son 32
Ho Chi Minh City
    51–53
Ho Chi Minh
    Trail 33
Hoi An 40
Hon Chong 44
Hué 33–38
Inland Route 42–43

Kim Lien 32
Lam Son 31
Lang Co 38
Lang Son 28–29
Mandarin Road
    31–33
Marble Mountain
    39
Mekong 57
Mekong Delta
    56–58
Meo Zao 28
My Son 41–42
My Tho 57–58
Nha Trang 43–46
Phan Thiet 49
Phong Nha 32
Perfume Pagoda,
    see Chua Huong
Po Klong Garai
    46–47
Po Nagar 44
Po Rome 47
Red River 23
Sa Pa 29
Saigon, see Ho Chi
    Minh City
Song Hong 23
Tay Ninh 54–55
Tay Phuong 24
Thanh Hoa 31
Vinh 31–32
Vung Tau 56
Water puppets 19
Waterfall Road
    48–49
Yok Don
    National Park 43

GENERAL EDITOR
    Barbara Ender-Jones
REVISED EDITION
    Martin Gostelow
LAYOUT
    Luc Malherbe
PHOTO CREDITS
    Bernard Joliat: pp. 13, 27;
    Renata Holzbachovà:
    pp. 1, 2, 6, 42, 49;
    Hémisphères/Rieger: p. 9;
    –/Frances: pp. 17, 37;
    –/Boisberranger: p. 21;
    –/Gardel: pp. 15, 24, 34, 45,
        50, 55, 60;
    –/Frilet: p. 39;
    Alice Delvaille: p. 10
MAPS
    Elsner & Schichor

Printed in Switzerland
Weber/Bienne (CTP) — 04/10/01
Edition 2005

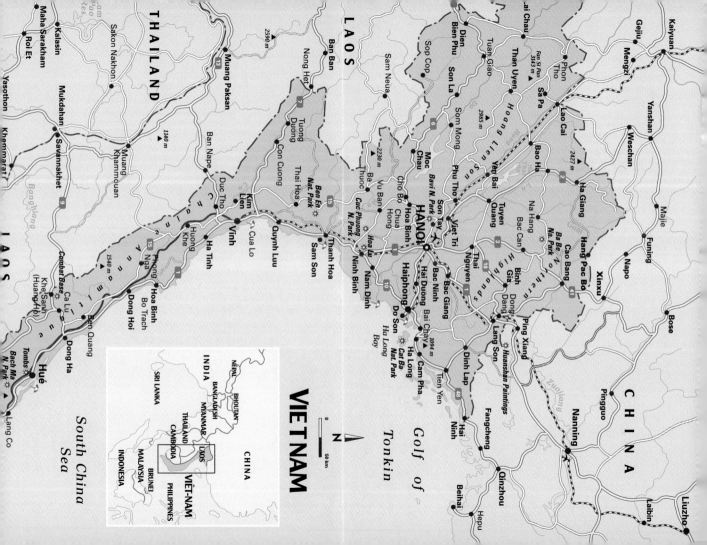

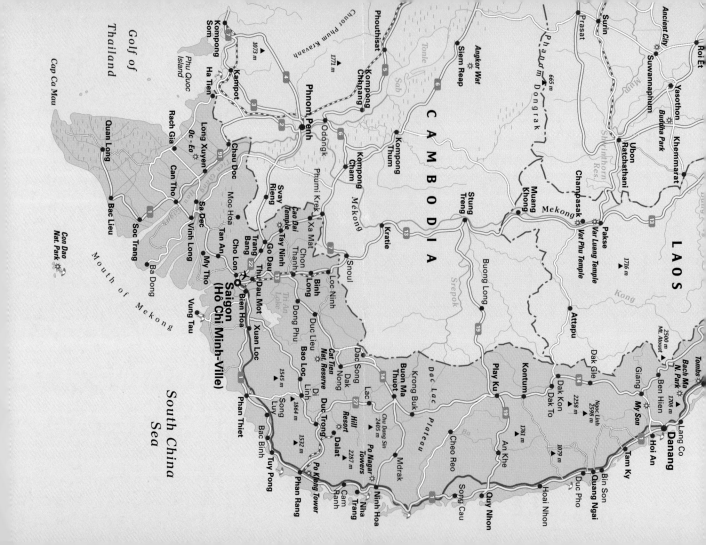

LAOS

Dan Colwell

JPMGUIDES

This Way Laos

A Million Elephants

This was once Lan Xang, the Kingdom of a Million Elephants. Enclosed by mountains, hemmed in by China, Vietnam, Cambodia, Thailand and Myanmar, it long remained a well-kept secret. The kingdom declined in the 19th century and was almost swallowed up by the Siamese empire, until the French took over the region and re-established the old borders along the Mekong River. In more recent times, the Vietnam War and a socialist revolution have conspired to wrench Laos out of the past.

An unshakeable otherworldliness remains, despite the transformation that has occurred since Laos began opening up to the outside world at the end of the 1980s. Many despise the plague of modernism, and throw up their hands in horror at the soulless, contemporary buildings that have sprouted on the city skylines. But the concept of modernity has always been relative here. Wander around the quiet streets of Luang Prabang in the early morning and you'll find that the peace of the former royal capital is broken only by the sound of gongs coming from ancient temples, or the soft sound of bare feet on stone, as saffron-robed Buddhist monks pad along in single file collecting alms from citizens seated cross-legged on the ground. Visit the country's most modern metropolis, Vientiane, and it will seem a sleepy little spot after the rumbustious mayhem of Phnom Penh or the economic dynamism of Bangkok. Wherever you find yourself in this land of beauty and tradition, the cultural ambience of Lan Xang never seems far away.

The Land

A long, thin sliver wedged into the middle of Indochina, Laos is topographically complex and entirely landlocked. It's slightly larger than Great Britain, which makes it extremely spacious in relation to its 6 million population, with a ratio of only 25 people per sq km. Given that 90 per cent of the land is mountainous, it's no surprise to find that the vast majority live along the banks of the Mekong. One of Asia's greatest rivers, the Mekong rises in Qinghai Province, China, and flows southwards through Tibet and into Laos, forming its border with Myanmar and Thailand. It then carries on to Vietnam and enters the South China Sea south of Ho Chi Minh City. The Mekong is the nation's lifeblood. The river irrigates the rice fields and yields abundant fish. In a country where the roads are difficult to navigate, it also serves as the main thoroughfare—at some point you'll almost inevitably find yourself sailing on the Mekong or one of its many scenic tributaries.

The People

For all the trials and tribulations of their recent history, you won't find a friendlier or more hospitable people than the citizens of Laos. Although their language will probably defeat you, one word you're sure to pick up quickly is *Sabaidee*—"welcome" or "hello", and always accompanied by a smile. Yet it's easy to get a mistaken impression about the cultural and ethnic unity of Laos. Visitors generally see only the people of the plains and the towns. In fact, just half the population are Lao Lum, or valley Lao, originally Tai migrants from southern China. The rest is made up of a patchwork of ethnic minorities, many of them living in the mountainous regions away from the main cities: the Lao Theung, or mountain Lao, of Indonesian origin; the Lao Sung, or uplands Lao; the Sino-Tibetan Hmong and Yao, and many others. Most Lao and some of the ethnic groups practice Theravada Buddhism—while many of the more remote hill people remain animists, or spirit worshippers. In the days of the monarchy, these groups formed a complex system of chiefdoms which recognized, more or less, the superiority of the king of Luang Prabang. More recently, some of the non-Lao groups—notably the Hmong—have rigorously resisted the Socialist government in Vientiane and continue to be a troublesome thorn in its side. How the Lao deal with their fellow-countrymen in the hills will be a test of whether or not their laid-back approach to life can be sustained in the years to come.

Flashback

Early Times

The history of Laos has been profoundly influenced by the actions and ambitions of neighbouring countries. From the 5th century AD, it was inhabited by a group of tribes known as the Kha, who were under the suzerainty of Funan, a powerful Hindu-Buddhist state based in what is now southern Cambodia and Vietnam. Some time around the 8th century, the Kha began to be supplanted by the Lao, a Tai-speaking branch of the tribes that controlled the kingdom of Nanchao in southwestern China. They soon established their own principalities and absorbed the local élites.

The Khmers

Throughout this period, Laos continued to be dominated by the great Khmer kingdom of Angkor, which had risen in northern Cambodia in the 9th century and reached its zenith in the 12th century. The Champasak province in the far south of Laos was part of the Angkorian empire itself, and

The amazing gold Wat Xieng Thong in Luang Prabang was built by King Setthathilat in 1559.

retains important buildings from that time.

Two vital changes came in the 13th century. Lao migration from China, which had been steadily rising over the years, rapidly increased when the Mongols under Kublai Khan destroyed Nanchao. And, as the Angkorian empire began to wane, Lao rulers had to face up to the new geopolitical reality in Indochina and pay tribute to the Siamese to the west. The fast-fading Khmers of Angkor had one last contribution to make to Lao history. In the mid-14th century they equipped the legendary Lao prince, Fa Ngum, with an army and sent him off to conquer the country.

Triumph of Fa Ngum

Nowadays, Fa Ngum is revered by Laotians as the founder of the nation. He had left Laos when young and was educated at the royal court in Angkor, later marrying the king's daughter. In 1351, he led his Khmer army into Laos from the top of a war-elephant. Two years later he fought his way to Muong Swa (now Luang Prabang) where he claimed the throne. He called the new kingdom Lan Xang and introduced Theravada Buddhism, 77 which was the state religion in Angkor. The warrior-king didn't stop there. For the next 20 years, Fa Ngum kept up a series of conquests, uniting all the Lao principalities in the process, and pushing his empire into northern and eastern Thailand.

Peace and War

Fa Ngum died in 1373, and his successors enjoyed 150 years of relative peace in which to establish the political order of Lan Xang. But the accession to the throne of Photisarath in 1520 marked a turn in the kingdom's fortunes. The ambition of Photisarath was to be a warrior-king in the mould of the great Fa Ngum, and he involved Lan Xang in a number of wars against Burma and the Thai kingdom of Ayutthaya. His aggressive policies managed to see his son placed on the throne of Chiang Mai in 1546, marking Lan Xang's furthest territorial expansion. But this imperial glory was short-lived. The king died two years later in an elephant-riding accident, and his son rushed back to rule as Setthathilat I, leaving Chiang Mai to be rapidly taken over by the Burmese. Lan Xang found itself on the defensive and soon under attack from its neighbours. Fearing the onslaught of the Burmese, Setthathilat moved the capital from Luang Prabang to Vien

Chan (now Vientiane) in 1563. The new capital was sacked twice in the next few years, and after the king's death in 1571, the Burmese conquered Vientiane. The kingdom was to remain in a state of chaos well into the next century.

The Lao Golden Age

From this grave position, the nation was about to enter its golden age. This was due primarily to the long reign and charismatic leadership of a new king, Souligna Vongsa, who ascended the throne in 1637 and remained in power for almost 60 years. A soldier, diplomat and patron of the arts, he fought successful wars against rebellious principalities, concluded peace treaties with Siam and Vietnam, and turned Vientiane into an important centre of Buddhist thought.

Division and Foreign Rule

When the king died in 1694, squabbles broke out over the succession. One of his nephews seized the throne with the backing of a Vietnamese army. In response, other members of the royal family, resentful of Vietnamese intrusion, established a separate kingdom in the old capital at Luang Prabang. Then in 1713, another kingdom was formed at Champasak in the south. The country was split into three, and the kingdom of Lan Xang effectively ceased to exist. Weakened and divided, the Lao became easy prey for larger neighbours, and during the 18th century the three kingdoms were annexed by Siam. The Lao kings were permitted to remain in place, but were no more than puppet rulers. So when King Anouvong thought himself strong enough to throw off the Siamese yoke and headed an army against Bangkok in 1827, it only led to the destruction of Vientiane a year later, and saw the region turned into a province of Siam.

Arrival of the French
Paradoxically, the territorial integrity of Laos was restored by the advent of another foreign conqueror in Indochina. France had concluded a first treaty with Vietnam in 1862, and so when the Siamese extended their military control of Laos towards the Vietnamese border, the French protested. It only took the threat of a showdown with the French to make the Siamese withdraw. In 1893, they sent a naval expedition to Bangkok, after which the frontier between Siam and French Indochina was established as the land east of the Mekong River—present-day Laos.

By 1904, the French had completed the annexation of the entire country, locating the administrative centre in Vientiane and allowing the monarch at Luang Prabang to keep his throne under the authority of a French resident supervisor.

Laos remained something of a colonial backwater until World War II, when in March 1945 the Japanese Army took full control from the wartime Vichy government. In response, the first Lao nationalist groups developed, and the nation was about to be transformed once again.

Independent Kingdom
Following the defeat of the Japanese, the French re-occupied the region and attempted to restore the old order. Hoping to marginalize the nationalist Lao Issara (Free Laos) movement, they set up King Sisavang Vong of Luang Prabang as the nominal ruler of a unified Laos within the French Union. But a new and more radical nationalism soon emerged. The Pathet Lao was created in 1950 under the leadership of Kaysone Phomvihan and Prince Souphanouvong, who was nicknamed the Red Prince in the West. They sided with the Vietminh against the French and gained power in northeast Laos. In the face of major military setbacks in the region, France finally withdrew from Indochina in 1954, and Laos became an independent kingdom.

79

Civil War

Throughout this time, the king's claim to represent a united nation was on shaky ground, as Pathet Lao forces continued to hold the northeastern provinces. The fragile peace ended in 1959 when civil war broke out between the Pathet Lao and the royal government. There was a temporary respite in 1962 during a short-lived coalition government that included both sides. But when the civil war got under way again two years later, it was as part of the greater regional conflict of the Vietnam War. The famous Ho Chi Minh Trail, running through northern Laos and used as a supply line by the North Vietnamese, became the target of US bombing raids; more than 2 million tonnes of explosives were dropped on eastern Laos in the years up to the end of the war.

Pathet Lao Seize Power

When the North Vietnamese defeated the US and marched into Saigon in April 1975, they began a chain-reaction of other communist takeovers in Indochina. The Khmer Rouge took control in Cambodia that same month, and shortly afterwards, in a bloodless coup, the Pathet Lao proclaimed the Lao People's Democratic Republic under President Souphanouvong—and the 600-year-old Lao monarchy was abolished.

Laos today

After the coup, the new government imitated the Vietnamese economic model and established a programme of collectivization in the countryside, nationalization of industry, and "re-education" camps for members of the former Lao military and political elite. As a consequence, up to 10 per cent of the population fled to Thailand. The Lao economy suffered dramatically, and so in 1980 private ownership was reintroduced. The links with Vietnam and the Soviet Union loosened after the end of the cold war in the late 1980s, and the building and development projects that are being carried out today are more likely to be funded by Japan, Australia and the international agencies. A new constitution enacted in 1991 permitted Laotians far greater freedom of movement at home and abroad.

The country is still one of the poorest in Asia and continues to be blighted by a vast quantity of unexploded bombs dropped by the Americans in the Vietnam War. But with Thailand now its main trading partner, and having secured membership of the Association of South-East Asia Nations (ASEAN) in 1997, Laos has begun to shake off its sense of isolation and looks to a future that's increasingly open to the world.

On the Scene

Vientiane is low-key by South-East Asian standards and serves as a perfect introduction to the easy-going Laotian way of life. Meanwhile, the number of historic sites at the ancient royal capital of Luang Prabang will keep the most dedicated culture-vultures busy for days. Both cities can be used as a base for side trips to places such as the great statue park of Xiang Khuan, or the Pak Ou Caves and their myriad Buddhas. Not to be missed is the mysterious Plain of Jars. For a taste of Laos at its most remote, and a glimpse of its fascinating hill tribes, it's worth trying to reach one or two of the outlying provinces, while in Champasak, in the far south, the ruins of the greatest Khmer temple outside Cambodia are sure to impress.

▶ VIENTIANE
City Centre, Around Vientiane, Beyond the City

Vientiane has been the capital of Laos since the 16th century. The city developed at the point where the first navigable reach of the Mekong flows out of the mountains and intersects with the road linking southern China and the Gulf of Thailand. It came under Siamese control in the 18th century, and was sacked in 1828 and the inhabitants deported. Many of its finest temples were destroyed, and little of what you see today predates the Siamese invasion. The city was still deserted when the French arrived in the 1860s,

and it was under French colonial rule that restoration work was carried out on important buildings such as That Luang.

Over the last few years, Vientiane has become a city of internet cafés, tourist hotels and international restaurants. Amazingly, this has happened without the place losing its laid-back and uniquely Lao character.

City Centre
Built on a curve of the Mekong, the city centre has a grid-plan layout, with the river to the south

and Nam Phou Place in the centre. It's very compact and easy to walk around, with plenty of pleasant bars and cafés.

Nam Phou Place

Though it's not exactly a Piccadilly Circus or Time Square, Nam Phou Place is as close to being a downtown hub as you're likely to find in Vientiane. It's marked by a fountain in the centre, while nearby are restaurants, a Scandinavian bakery, tourist agencies and hotels. At the south end runs Setthathilat Road, a delightful tree-lined boulevard which contains some of the city's finest temples.

Lao National Museum

In a French colonial dwelling on Samsenthai Road north of Nam Phou Place, this used to be known as the Lao Revolutionary Museum. The old name tells you much about the displays inside. A few rooms take in archaeological finds, anthropological information on Laos's ethnic groups and the history of the kingdom of Lan Xang, but the bulk of the museum is devoted to artefacts and photos documenting the Pathet Lao's struggle for power against the French, the Americans and the royalist government. In this light, it's a fascinating relic from the Cold War era, where you can see items such as Comrade Souphan-ouvong's table, at which the Red Prince developed his plans to create a revolution, or photos and paintings captioned with suitably anti-Western propaganda.

Presidential Palace and Colonial Quarter

Follow Setthathilat Road eastwards from Nam Phou Place and you'll come to the colonial splendour of the Presidential Palace. It stands on the site of the former royal palace, and was occupied in succession by the French Resident during the protectorate, the king of reunified Laos, and latterly the president of the Lao Republic.

The administrative part of town huddles around the palace. Just beyond it is the old colonial quarter, with several other buildings dating from the time of the French Protectorate. In particular, look out for the cathedral, the hospital and the French embassy, all of which give some idea of the colonial style of architecture that the French brought to Indochina.

Wat Haw Phra Kaew

Next door, this temple was the chapel of the royal palace. It was restored by prince Suvanna Phuma and transformed into a remarkable museum of religious art. The chapel was built during the 1560s to shelter the *Phra Kaew*, or Emerald Buddha, but this was carried off by the Siamese in 1778 and is still held in Bangkok. Apart from the fabulous sculpted doors and golden throne, you'll see an impressive collection of Buddhas going back to the 6th century. Images of Buddha are always carved in stylized postures called *mudra*. The "Calling for Rain" posture is typically Lao; it depicts the Buddha standing with his hands held rigidly at each side, fingers pointing to the ground. Look out too for an 18th-century throne in the form of a *naga*, a mythical serpent. In the garden is one of the famous great stone jars, transported by helicopter from the Plain of Jars.

Wat Si Saket

Opposite the Presidential Palace, this is the residence of the Buddhist community, Phra Sangka Nagnok. It was built in 1818 by King Anouvong and spared from destruction by the Siamese attack ten years later, possibly because it was designed in a Siamese architectural style.

The main sanctuary (*sim*) is packed with hundreds of Buddhas in all sizes and of all materials. Note the outstanding Naga Buddha in Khmer style, seated beneath a canopy formed by a multi-headed *naga*, and the 19th-century murals depicting episodes from the reincarnated lives of the Buddha. The coffered ceil-

---

THE WAT

It's not simply a temple or a monastery. A wat is at once a place of worship, a school, a hospital and a meeting place. All wats are built on the same pattern. Between the outer and inner walls are the monks' dormitories (*kutis*), a belltower (*haw rakang*) and a library (*haw trai*), where Buddhist scriptures are stored. The inner wall separates the sacred and the profane, and often takes the form of a cloister lined with images of Buddha, to encourage meditation. In the courtyard, the rectangular *viharn* is an assembly hall. Reserved for the monks, the temple, *sim*, houses the main image of Buddha. The *sim* itself is surrounded by stone tablets, or boundary markers, placed at the principal and intermediate points of the compass. A number of chambers (*that*), in the form of lotus buds, contain holy relics of Buddha or the ashes of royalty, dignitaries or monks. Some wats also have a *haw phi khun*, or spirit house, for the temple's reigning earth spirit. Though the worship of spirits has been banned, the Lao still make offerings to these guardians of people or places.

ing of the great hall is decorated with a floral motif inspired by the Thai temples of Ayutthaya, said to be influenced in turn by the decor of Louis XIV's palace in Versailles. Behind the *sim*, a long wooden trough sculpted in the form of a *naga* serves at New Year when the images of Buddha are sprinkled with holy water for ritual cleansing.

Wat Si Muang

Further east along Setthathilat Road, the lower town still retains something of a village atmosphere. The heart of this area is dominated by Wat Si Muang, at the main crossroads. This is the site of the city pillar, *lak muang*, and is thus considered the home of Vientiane's guardian spirit. According to legend, when the hole was dug for the pillar, a pregnant girl jumped in and the ropes were released, her sacrifice establishing the town guardianship. Today, it's a bright, bustling temple, with a continual stream of worshippers from the local community, and numerous street stalls outside selling saffron, candles and other items to make up offerings to the shrine.

Wat Ong Teu

Head back towards the stretch of Setthathilat Road west of Nam Phou Place, with its string of attractive monasteries. Surrounded by the residences of high-ranking families and set in a delightful garden, Wat Ong Teu is known for its enormous bronze Buddha. Cast in the 16th century, the statue weighs several tons—indeed, Wat Ong Teu means the "Temple of the Heavy Buddha". This is an especially lively place to be in November when the That Luang festival is celebrated here, dating from the times when the nobles swore allegiance to the king and constitution.

Along the Mekong River

Follow any street south from the city centre and you come to Fa Ngum Road, which runs alongside the Mekong. The riverside here provides a pleasant place for a late-afternoon stroll—the land on the opposite bank is Thailand. It also has great sunset views and is lined with bars and foodstalls at which to enjoy them.

Around Vientiane

A new and more expansive town has sprung up outside the ancient fortifications. Unless you're a dedicated city-walker you will probably want to take a taxi from the centre to places such as the Patuxai arch and the historic That Luang temple.

Lan Xang Avenue

Leading from the Presidential Palace up to a large triumphal

The spire of That Luang, the Great Sacred Stupa, represents a lotus bud, topped by a stylized banana flower and an umbrella.

arch, this wide boulevard self-consciously evokes the Champs-Elysées in Paris, though it's certainly a fairly run-down version. Here you'll find banks, the main post office, the tourist information bureau and the Morning Market, known as Talat Sao. This vast affair is surprisingly hassle-free compared to most South-East Asian markets, and is filled with stalls selling jewellery, textiles, clothes, electronic goods and souvenirs.

Patuxai Arch

At the top of Lan Xang Avenue, the Patuxai, also called Anusa-wali ("Monument") is a triumph-al arch built to commemorate the Lao who died in the pre-Revolutionary wars. Though inspired by the Arc de Triomphe in Paris, it incorporates Lao architectural and decorative motifs. Work began on it in 1958, and it's said to have been completed using concrete initially intended by the Americans for expanding the airport—locals have nicknamed it the "vertical runway". For good views of the city, you can climb the stairway to the top.

That Luang

A 15-minute walk east of Patuxai, the Great Sacred Stupa is the national place of pilgrimage, the 85 most venerated Buddhist monument in the country. Built by King Setthathilat in 1566 on the site of a Khmer temple, it was restored by a French university department in the 1930s. In ritual worship, the faithful have to make their way along the two terraces, from left to right, to reach the golden stupa, crowned by a spire in the form of an elongated lotus bud. During the fierce daytime sunlight the stupa is almost too dazzling to look at, and is seen to best effect at sunset or at the time of the That Luang Festival, of which this shrine is the focus.

Beyond the City

Outside the capital there are several interesting places to visit, ranging from the eccentricities of a Buddhist theme park to the atmospheric karst caves in the Lao countryside around Vang Vieng. They can be reached by bus, but if you prefer to be more independent, hiring a taxi will not break the bank.

Suan Vathanatham

Located 20 km (12 miles) downstream of Vientiane, the National Ethnic Culture Park contains a rich assortment of attractions, including replicas of traditional Lao houses, concrete dinosaurs, a small zoo, bars, restaurants and views of the Friendship Bridge.

Wat Xieng Khuan

A further 4 km (2.5 miles) away, Wat Xieng Khuan is not really a wat. Created in the 1950s and 60s by a monk, Luang Pu Bunleua Sulilat, it's a sort of mystical garden cum religious theme park, planted with a bizarre assortment of cement sculptures representing various divinities that include Shiva, Vishnu and Buddha. You can get an overview of the park by climbing to the top of a large structure that's meant to represent the three levels of existence—hell, earth and heaven. It's undoubtedly unusual and all rather kitsch. In case you're moved to wonder about the park's creator, Luang Pu fled to Thailand after the Pathet Lao came to power, and built another one there.

Vang Vieng

A peaceful town 156 km (97 miles) north of Vientiane, Vang Vieng is scenically located on the banks of the Nam Xong river. It's set among limestone karst hills perforated by a series of caves. The best-known and most accessible of these is Tham Chang, where you can see intriguing rock formations, swim in a stream and enjoy great views over the valley from its mouth. The caves a little further out, such as Tham Phou Kam and Tham Xang offer spectacular karst scenery and a dramatic sense of isolation.

The former royal capital is a small town surrounded by lush, green mountains, where the Khan river flows into the Mekong. It has been at the heart of Lao culture ever since Fa Ngum established it as the capital of Lan Xang in 1353. Known for the next two centuries by its original name of Muong Swa, it acquired its current name under King Setthathilat in 1563 in honour of the Pra Bang, a Sri Lankan-made gold Buddha brought here by Fa Ngum from Angkor. That same year, the king relocated the capital to Vientiane. The town had a new lease of life as a royal capital in 1707, when Lan Xang disintegrated and the kingdom of Luang Prabang emerged. A proud tradition of Lao music and dance, architecture, craftsmanship and haute cuisine grew up around the court. Although the royal connection ended with the Pathet Lao revolution of 1975, the city remains a fascinating compendium of traditional Lao culture, both sacred and profane.

The Old City
The old city of Luang Prabang is enclosed in a curve traced by the Khan, the northern part forming a long peninsula. In the centre is a large hill, the Phu Si, a perfect symbol of a cosmic mountain emerging from the waters. Around this is the magnificent royal palace, a host of beautiful sloping-roof temples, and numerous ancient lanes and alleyways. Be sure to get out by 6 a.m. on at least one morning, when you'll find rows of saffron-robed monks silently collecting alms. Certainly, it's a place rich in atmosphere, and steeped in the history of the country's glorious past.

Royal Palace
Located between Phu Si hill and the Mekong, the former Royal Palace was rebuilt by the French as a permanent structure in 1904, during the reign of King Sisavang Vong, and topped by a graceful Lao-style spire a quarter of a century later. It's made up of three embedded parts: the reception rooms, the throne room, and the private chambers. The palace was converted into a museum in 1976, a year after the last king of Laos was sent into exile.

The collections include classical instruments, masks used for performances of the *Ramayana*, paintings of Luang Prabang executed by the French artist Alex de Fautereau in 1930, numerous religious objects and mementoes of the monarchy. There's also a 87

The Royal Palace, a humble building enshrining magnificent treasures.

room devoted to the diplomatic gifts presented to Laos, grouped according to the politics of the donating countries, capitalist or socialist. The most prized work of art in the museum is the Pra Bang, a standing statue of the Buddha said to be made of solid gold, and which gave its name to the city. It's kept in a purpose-built shrine near the entrance to the palace, and is said by some to be a copy, with the original stored away in a bank vault.

Wat Mai

Next to the palace, Wat Mai (or Wat Mai Suwannaphumaham, to give it its full name) was the resi-

dence of the Sangkhalat, the highest dignitary of the Lao Buddhist church. The temple dates from the late 18th century, and serves as a chapel for the palace. During the lively New Year celebrations it becomes the scene of a ritual baptism of the Pra Bang. On the front veranda, the superb gold relief door panels tell the story of Pra Wet, the penultimate reincarnation of Buddha.

Chinatown

It's worth looking round the neighbouring district, which boasts several traditional residences, notably the home of Prince Tiao Sayavong. The area

THE OLD CITY ◀

just to the north of the palace is also known as *Ban Jek*, or Chinatown. Many of the shops here are run by people of Chinese origin, while the 19th-century Wat Chum Khong has two statues of the Chinese Bodhisattva, testifying to the longstanding relations between Luang Prabang and its great northern neighbour.

Phu Si

Opposite the Royal Palace is the Phu Si hill. You can climb up the 328 steps to the top, where you'll be rewarded with great views of the town, as well as the rivers and jungle-covered mountains that surround it. This is also a very popular place at sunset. The hill was covered in temples in the 18th century, but there are only five left. That Chom Si, built in 1804 crowns the summit, and is the starting-point for the torch-lit procession at Lao New Year in April.

Wat Aham
and Wat Wisunalat

Behind Phu Si, away from the main part of town, are some stunning views of the Nam Khan river and the hills beyond. If you continue on the road south, keeping the Nam Khan on your left, you'll come to two of the city's finest temples.

Wat Aham encloses the shrine of the royal spirit protector, Haw Phi Khon, at the base of two large bodhi trees. Immediately next to it, Wat Wisunalat (or Visoun), is renowned for its collection of religious art which includes a number of Buddhas in the "Calling for Rain" posture. The original wooden temple was built in 1512, but marauding Chinese Ho burned it to the ground in 1887.

In front of the temple, That Pathum, the Lotus Stupa, is built in the shape of a watermelon. Also known as That Makmo, the 34.5-m (113-ft) structure was built by order of Nang Phantin Xieng, wife of King Wisun, at the beginning of the 16th century. The stupa's unusual shape recalls the mythological origins of the Lao culture: the legend recounts that a certain Khun Bulom cut open a gourd somewhere near Dien Bien Phu (in Vietnam) and out sprang seven sons who spread the Thai-Lao family east and west.

Wat Xieng Thong

Near the tip of the peninsula, overlooking the Mekong, the magnificent Wat Xieng Thong was the city's most important royal temple and ranks as one of the richest artistic achievements in Laos. It was built by King Setthathilat in 1560. The *sim* is in classic Luang Prabang style, with a stunning tiered roof and gilt murals on its black exterior walls. 89

Enter through decorated doors to the dark interior, whose columns, beams and walls are covered in superb gold-leaf murals.

Just behind the *sim* is a small shrine with a striking mosaic design and a standing Buddha inside. Look out too for the Red Chapel, with its highly regarded sculpture of a reclining Buddha.

Across the courtyard is the modern Funerary Carriage Hall, containing the royal funeral carriages and urns, together with a small collection of puppets, currency and other mementoes from the royalist era.

Wat Pakkhan

Not far from Wat Xieng Thong, this temple is close to the mouth of the Nam Khan; the king used to watch the royal regattas from its platform. Dating from the 18th century, its handsome doors reveal a Chinese influence.

The Lower Town

Lesser mortals lived—and still do—in the lower town, where you'll discover the markets and countless artisans, with the silversmiths bunched together down by the river. The district boasts some of the city's oldest and finest temples—Buddhism was late coming to Luang Prabang and at first was restricted to this area.

Wat That, or Wat Pha Mahathat, sits at the top of a staircase with a *naga* balustrade and has some outstanding woodcarvings on the façade.

Further out, Wat That Luang was built at the beginning of the 19th century and contains the ashes of members of the royal family. The gold stupa at one end of the compound is the mausoleum of the last king of Laos.

Around Luang Prabang

There are some intriguing places of interest close to the city. They can be easily reached either by road or scenic Mekong river boat rides.

Across the Mekong

Plenty of ferries are on hand to take you across the river. On the riverbank, Wat Long Khoum is where each new king of Luang Prabang would spend a three-day retreat before his coronation. The red, blue and gold carved doors of the temple are especially noteworthy.

Not far from here, Wat Tham is located inside a cave 100-m (328 ft) deep. It contains vast quantities of old Buddhas, though it isn't lit, so you'll need to bring a torch if you want to see anything. Climb the path to Wat Chom Phet. The temple is no longer in use and there are tales of spirits haunting the place—but it also offers unparalleled sunset views of Luang Prabang.

Pak Ou Caves

Boats can be hired from the pier in front of the Royal Palace to the caves, about 25 km (15 miles) upstream along the Mekong. The setting is delightful in itself but also holds symbolic interest. In a triple-peak mountain landscape at the confluence of the Mekong and the Ou, two caves—Tham Thing and Tham Phum—burrow into a limestone cliff. They represent the womb of the earth, out of which trickle the first waters of life, irrigating and purifying the land. These caves are particularly revered by the Lao, as you can see from the offerings of thousands of Buddhas that have accumulated over the centuries.

Kouang Si Waterfall

Located about 30 km (18 miles) to the west of Luang Prabang, these picturesque falls are a great place to avoid the midday heat. With a 60-m (196-ft) drop over jutting rocks, the spray keeps the area refreshingly cool, and there are also plenty of small pools that are delightful for swimming. Bear in mind that this is a popular weekend picnic spot with the locals and can get very crowded; during the week you'll find it a haven of peace. The falls can be reached by river or road. This last route allows you to see villages inhabited by ethnic groups such as the Hmong and Lao Theung.

Plain of Jars

This vast, mysterious plain in Xieng Khuang Province, 12 km (7 miles) south of Phonsavan, is scattered with hundreds of huge stone jars gaping towards the heavens. In varying sizes, they measure up to 2.5 m (8 ft) tall, and the biggest weighs a hefty 6 tons. Here and there lie big stone lids. Adding to the mystery is the fact that the stone was not quarried locally, and no one knows how it was transported here. Moreover, tools and bronze ornaments were discovered in this area, left by a civilization that has not yet been identified—some anthropologists believe they are the traces of a lost Indochinese people. A number of different theories have been proposed as to the purpose of these jars: perhaps they were sarcophagi, or maybe they were used for storing grain or fermenting wine.

When you go exploring, do not stray too far off the main paths without a reliable guide. During the Vietnam War, this area was fought over by government forces, Pathet Lao insurgents and North Vietnamese troops, as well as being intensively bombed by the Americans. There's still a considerable amount of unexploded ordnance here. Miraculously, however, most of the jars escaped damage.

91

Savannakhet

On the banks of the Mekong, Savannakhet stands at the crossroads of road 13 to the far south, and road 9 eastwards to Vietnam. Commonly known as Savan, the town was founded by the French and has an attractive colonial quarter around the town square. The shrine of the city's guardian spirit looks out over the river, but the main temple, Wat Sayaphum, stands on the landward side of the road running along the river bank, sheltering the municipality's ceremonial boat.

In an old colonial mansion, the provincial museum has displays on local boy Kaysone Phomvihane, one of the founders of Pathet Lao, and relics dating from the time of the Vietnam War.

Ban That

At the village of Ban That, north of Savan, That Ing Hang is of Khmer inspiration; it is considered to be the holiest religious building in southern Laos. Three superimposed terraces are topped by the traditional Lao stupa and a gold umbrella. Many of the sculptures are erotic, recalling one of the symbolic meanings of the stupa: the image of a phallus reaching towards the fecund heavens.

Champasak Province

After the Khemmarat rapids, the Mekong flows peacefully for 200 km (120 miles) before tumbling into the Khon Phapheng Falls. The basin forms a distinctive region with a complicated history. It was part of the Angkor empire from the 10th to the 13th centuries, then was incorporated into the Lan Xang kingdom, breaking away to become the autonomous principality of Champasak in 1713. Parts were whittled away by Siam, and the remainder was integrated into French Indochina, though the people remained faithful to the local monarchy. In 1946, when Laos was reunified, the crown prince Chao Bounome renounced his rights to the throne, but he was able to maintain the ritual and symbolic apparatus of his ancestry. Until, that is, the Communists took power. The prince had to flee to Paris, where he died in 1978.

Pakse

The bustling regional capital lies at the confluence of the Mekong and the Xe Don. Prince Bounome started building a five-storey palace here in 1968 but never had time to finish it. It has now been converted into a hotel. You might also want to check out the provincial museum, which has interesting examples of Khmer art as well as jewellery and costumes from Laos's ethnic groups, alongside the inevitable displays devoted to the triumph of the Pathet Lao revolution.

Ban Saphai

A short distance from Pakse on the west bank of the Mekong, Ban Saphai village is well known for maintaining traditional hand-weaving techniques. You can watch the weavers work at their looms, and purchase the silk textiles they produce here.

Bolovens Plateau

This high plateau to the east of Pakse provides welcome relief from the searing heat of the Mekong valley. Its fertile red soil, of volcanic origin, has been farmed intensively since the French first introduced coffee, rubber and bananas in the early 20th century. Now strawberries and raspberries, cardamom and rattan are also grown here. The main town, Paksong, was virtually destroyed in the war.

The Bolovens plateau and the area of Saravan to the north are home to a score of Mon-Khmer minority groups, including the Alak, Ya Houne, Ta-Oy and Katang. Treks to Alak and Katang villages are a great way of seeing

the countryside, and local buses run to places such as the spectacular Tad Lo and Tad Farn waterfalls.

Wat Phu

On the right bank of the Mekong, 30 km (18 miles) south of Pakse, is a hill 75 m (246 ft) high and shaped like an immense *lingam*, the phallic symbol of Shiva. The site has been sacred since prehistoric times, and it's thought that human sacrifices were carried out here. The present temple, Wat Phu, is of Khmer origin—possibly dating originally from the pre-Angkorian era of the 5th or 6th century, but completed by Suryavarman II, the 12th-century king who built the great Angkor Wat in northern Cambodia.

It is built on megalithic terraces from the 1st millennium BC. The three main levels are linked by a processional causeway which would once have been flanked by statues of lions and mythical beasts. On the uppermost level, the main sanctuary once housed a large lingam that was washed by water channelled from the holy spring flowing from a cave at the top of the hill. Here, the views over the ancient temple complex and the mysterious jungle that encloses it are breathtaking.

Khon Phapheng Falls

Near the Cambodian border, the Mekong breaks up into a tangle of channels and waterfalls, forming hundreds of islands. The Khon Phapheng falls, 160 km (100 miles) downstream from Pakse, are the largest cascades in a 13-km (8-mile) stretch of powerful rapids—indeed, they are the largest falls in South-East Asia. There's a wooden pavilion on the riverbank for viewing them: the bamboo scaffolding on the rocks is used by local fishermen who benefit from divine protection by the spirits of the falls.

THE BACI

For important events in family life (a journey, illness, birth, and so on), the Lao hold a ceremony called the *baci*, or *sukwan*. The neighbours gather around a tray laden with fruit, eggs, sweetmeats and flowers, arranged in the form of a cosmic mountain, from which dangle 32 cotton strings. An official recites a prayer to summon the 32 *kwan* (guardian spirits) that rule over a person's body. Once the *kwan* have settled on the mountain of offerings, the guests tie the strings round their wrists to retain them, and make wishes. The offerings are shared out, then the dancing and merry-making can begin.

Shopping

Once you have brushed aside the tourist trash, you'll discover that Laos is a nation of skilled craftsmen, producing great-value hand-crafted goods using materials such as textiles and silver.

If you're travelling beyond the main cities, you can buy locally made items in the villages themselves or at provincial markets. Otherwise, scout around Vientiane's vast Morning Market or the Dala Market in Luang Prabang for a wide range of Laotian handicrafts. Luang Prabang also has a Hmong market, selling goods made by the hill people of Northern Laos.

Textiles
Rough-textured fabrics of silk or cotton are a Lao speciality. The dominant colour is navy, interwoven with traditional designs whose origins are lost in the mists of time. Every ethnic group, every province has its distinctive patterns. In general, the lengths are made up in standard sizes for a skirt (*sin*) or a scarf, wall hangings or bed covers.

There's also a tradition of "aristocratic" weaving: a smooth silk intended for clothes worn for ceremonious occasions or going to the temple. These fabrics are lighter in colour, in faded or pastel tones, sometimes shot through with gold threads. Particular attention is paid to the strip forming the hem of the *sin*.

Silverware
Lao jewellery is generally made of silver and sold by weight. It is divided into two styles: that of the hill tribes and that of the plains. You'll see belts, bracelets, anklets and necklaces on show. There are also silverware items like decorated boxes and bowls, as well as animal and human figures. With a bit of patience you can find articles of exceptional purity and beauty, especially in Luang Prabang, where the tradition of the royal silversmiths has managed to survive the end of the monarchy.

Other handicrafts
Wooden objects can range from sculpted images of the Buddha to ornately carved pipes. Traditional village craftsmen favour materials like rattan, wicker and bamboo, which make excellent baskets, bowls, kitchen utensils and mats, as well as furniture.

Dining Out

Closer in spirit to Thai rather than Chinese or Vietnamese cooking, the distinctive taste of Lao cuisine is created with flavours such as lime juice, fresh coriander, lemon grass, chillies and fermented fish sauces. Main ingredients include chicken, beef and pork, although the favoured traditional food is freshwater fish.

Home Cooking

Lao cuisine is frequently fiery and always piquant, so the perfect accompaniment is rice and a glass of excellent Lao-brewed beer. However, there are not many Lao restaurants—Chinese and Vietnamese establishments are in far greater supply. It's often said that to find the best Lao food you have to be invited to someone's home. European and American cuisine is well represented in the main cities these days, with some truly first-rate French cooking now to be found in Vientiane and Luang Prabang.

The Basics

The Lao are rice eaters. The grain is a particularly appetizing variety, improperly known as glutinous, or sticky rice, *khao nio*. It does not grow in great quantity, but is very nutritious. To prepare it, the rice is soaked for several hours, then steamed and served in little baskets. You take up a portion with four fingers and form it into a little ball, which you dip into the accompanying dishes.

Rice is generally served with *padek*, a pungent concoction of fish macerated in wheat germ and salt. *Kin khao kap padek*, literally "to eat sticky rice and padek", is the staple peasant meal.

The other staple guaranteed to gladden the heart of any Lao is noodles, mainly eaten for breakfast in a spicy broth called *foe*. You'll also come across *khao pun*, which is an extremely popular noodle dish served with an assortment of raw vegetables and seasoned with a meat, fish and coconut sauce; and a chicken-and-ginger version, *khao biak sen*. These are best enjoyed at atmospheric, down-to-earth street stalls and noodle shops.

Main courses

A serious contender for the title of Lao national dish, *lap* is a banquet meal of minced raw beef or venison mixed with aubergine, chilli, fish sauce, garlic and shallots. It's run a close second by the tasty green papaya salad, *tam mak houng*, consisting of shredded green papaya, chilli, garlic and lime juice.

Soups will be brought with the other main dishes, as they are not considere as starters. Try *gaeng pag nam*, made from watercress; *tom yam pa*, a fish, lemon grass and mushroom soup; or *gaeng jeut*, with pork and vegetables.

Also on the menu might be *goy moo*, pork salad with fresh herbs; *kali kai*, a spicy chicken curry; *phanang-kai*, chicken with peanut stuffing; and *sa ton pa*, raw fish chopped and spiced with a complicated sauce.

A real treat if you're in Luang Prabang is *mok pa*, steamed fish in banana leaves. Other possibilities include *tom-pon* and *o-pa*, both based on boiled fish pepped up with spices; *mu-nem*, minced pork with lettuce; *sin-heng*, dried buffalo or venison; *khua*, meat sautéed with garlic and onions; *roy tium*, fish parcels; and *som khay*, a type of caviar.

For dessert, you might find some restaurants offering *ngoon kati*, coconut jelly, or *nam wan mak kuay*, banana in coconut milk.

Delicious when mangoes are in season, *khao niaw mak muang* is a sort of rice pudding with mango and coconut.

Drinks

The French began growing coffee on the Bolovens Plateau in southern Laos in the early 20th century—the Lao like to take it very strong and very sweet.

Fruit juices and sweetened fruit shakes are popular, and available at street stalls and shops throughout every town.

The Lao's favourite tipple is *lao-lao*, a strong spirit made from rice. Some villages are reputed for the quality of their *lao-lao*, such as the one halfway between Luang Prabang and the Pak Ou Caves. Locally brewed Beer Lao, light in colour, is delicious with spicy Lao food.

The Hard Facts

Airports

Wattay International Airport is situated 6 km (4 miles) west of Vientiane; Luang Prabang Airport is a mere 2 km east of the ancient capital. The terminals have cafés, currency exchange and duty-free facilities.

If you do not already have special arrangements made for the journey into town (some hotels offer a free pick-up service), you'll find plenty of taxis outside the terminal buildings.

You will have to pay a departure tax on international and domestic flights.

Climate

Laos has a tropical climate, with a monsoon season bringing heavy rains between May and September, and a dry season from October to April. The coolest period is between November and January, when average temperatures get down to a comfortable 28°C (82°F), though in the highlands it can become very cold indeed at this time; the hottest is April, with temperatures regularly reaching 36°C (96.8°F).

Communications

The postal service in Laos is efficient and reliable. As well as selling stamps and phonecards, the main post offices in Vientiane and Luang Prabang offer telephone, fax and post restante facilities. The post office in Vientiane is on the corner of Khou Viang Road and Lan Xang Avenue; in Luang Prabang it's on Chao Fa Ngum Road, diagonally across from the Hmong Market.

International telephone calls are cheaper if made at the post office rather than from your hotel. Lao Telecom phonecards can be purchased from shops and hotels as well as the post office. The international access code is 00, followed by the country code, 1 for USA and Canada, 44 for UK, 61 for Australia, then the area code (minus initial zero) and the local number. The country code for Laos if you are dialling from abroad is 856; the city code for Vientiane is 021; Luang Prabang is 071.

Faxes can be sent and received at hotels, but are expensive. The internet is very popular in Laos, and is by far the cheapest way of keeping in touch with people at home. There are plenty of Internet cafés in the main cities, and still easily found elsewhere in the country. Larger hotels also offer this facility.

Driving

Foreign tourists are permitted to rent cars and motorbikes. However, given the difficult driving conditions that prevail here, it's usually a more stress-free option as well as less expensive to hire a car with a driver. This will probably be a necessity if you want to get to any out-of-the-way places, as public transport is very slow. Car hire can be arranged through your hotel or a reputable travel agent.

Emergencies

Most problems can be handled at your hotel desk. If you have a medical problem, there are various clinics in Vientiane that can offer an international standard of healthcare. To call an ambulance dial 195.

The Australian Clinic at the Australian Embassy is open 24 hours a day, tel. 021 413 603 or 021 413 610; it accepts Canadian, American and English patients. There's an International Medical Clinic at the Mahosat Hospital Centre, tel. 021 315 015, though this is only open in the morning. There are also clinics at the French and Swedish embassies.

For more serious emergencies the Trauma Centre at the Friendship Hospital is open 24 hours a day, tel. 021 413 302. As a last resort, emergency transfers by helicopter to the Udon Thani Hospital in Thailand can be arranged through Westcoast Helicopter, tel. 021 512 023. This is inevitably a very expensive service, so check whether you are covered by your insurance.

Formalities

You will need a passport, valid for at least six months before its expiry date. Tourist visas valid for 15 days are issued on arrival and cost US$30. Remember to bring a passport-size photo of yourself—if not, you pay an extra US$2 for your passport to be photocopied. Laos embassies in the US, Australia, France or Germany, among others, can issue 15- or 30-day visas at varying costs. There is no Laos embassy in the UK, but officially recognized tour companies should be able to obtain a visa for you.

Health

Before you leave be sure to buy travel insurance that includes medical cover, and have all the necessary immunizations—contact your doctor or travel centre to find out what's required. You'll also need to start taking a course of antimalarial tablets prior to departure. Preventing the insects getting to you is best, though, so it's a good idea to take mosquito repellent, and keep your arms and legs covered in the evenings if possible.

99

With a little care you should encounter no health problems during your stay. It's wise to avoid too much exposure to the sun. Wear a hat, use a good sunscreen and keep in the shade as much as possible, especially in the middle of the day. Drink plenty of mineral water to avoid dehydration—never tap water. In the same vein, do not eat salad or fruit that has been washed in unpurified water, and beware of ice cubes and fruit juice diluted with tap water—indeed, it's even worth brushing your teeth in mineral water.

If you require specialized prescription medicines, remember to take enough with you to last for the duration of your stay.

Holidays and Festivals
Many of Laos's public holidays and festivals follow the lunar calendar, and so move from year to year. During all of the following public holidays and most of the festivals, you'll find banks and offices shut.

January 1	New Year's Day
January 6	Pathet Lao Day
January 20	Army Day
March 8	International Women's Day
March 22	Lao People's Party Day
May 1	International Labour Day
June 1	International Children's Day
August 13	*Lao Issara* (independence of the Lao people)
August 23	Liberation Day (from the French)
October 12	Liberation Day
December 2	Independence Day (parades and plenty of flag-waving)

Moveable festivals:
Dec–Jan: *Boun Pha Wet* celebrates the penultimate incarnation of the Buddha with music and dancing.

March: *Boun Khoun Khao* is thanksgiving.

Mid-April: *Boun Pimai*, the Lao New Year, is a time of processions and riotous merry-making, like Thailand's Songkran.

May: *Boun Bang Fai* is known as the Rocket Festiva: fireworks are fired heavenwards to induce rainfall.

June/July: *Khao Pansa* is the beginning of the Buddhist Lent.
August: *Ho Khao Padap Dinh*, All Saints Day.

Sept/Oct: *Bouk ok Pansa* signals the end of the Buddhist Lent.
October: *Boun Lay Heua Phai* is a colourful water festival with boat races, celebrating the end of the rainy season.

Oct–Nov: the three-day *That Luang* festival is centred around the That Luang temple in Vientiane.

Many shops and offices also close for the Chinese and Vietnamese New Year in January or February.

Language

Lao is the official language of Laos. One of the Tai languages of South-East Asia, it's closely related to that spoken in neighbouring Thailand. It's mainly monosyllabic and uses tones to differentiate between words—which means that Lao is fiendishly difficult for Westerners to learn. Luckily, English is widely understood, especially by younger people in urban areas, while French might come in useful with older Laotians.

Media

There is only one locally published foreign-language newspaper, the bi-weekly *Vientiane Times*, which isn't exactly a sparkling read but does offer some insight into the day-to-day life of the nation. It has a website, www.vientianetimes.com.

International newspapers other than *The Bangkok Post* are hard to come by, though you might find some old copies of *Asiaweek* and *Time* on sale in bookshops.

Most medium- and top-range hotels have satellite TV, showing channels like CNN and MTV.

Short-wave radio enthusiasts can listen to BBC World Service, Voice of America and Radio Australia, but be sure to check the times and frequencies before you leave, as they often change.

Money matters

The unit of currency is the *kip* (K), which comes in notes of 50, 100, 500, 1000, 2000 and 5,000. There are no coins. In recent years the *kip* has been subject to the effects of high inflation, and you'll find that the US dollar is not only used as the benchmark for prices, but also as a day to day part of the Lao monetary system. Thai *baht* are also generally accepted.

This is very much a cash economy, although credit cards are taken at many tourist hotels and restaurants in the larger cities these days. Bring enough money in low denomination US dollar bills and US dollar travellers cheques to cover such things as meals, travel and shopping for the duration of your holiday. You can obtain cash advances on credit cards at banks and exchange bureaux, but doing so will incur heavy charges. There are no ATMs (cash machines).

If you do bring other currencies, make sure you don't change too much into *kip* at any one time: you'll acquire plenty of them in your small change anyway, but 101 more importantly it isn't a convertible currency; banks and exchange bureaux won't buy it back from you when you leave the country.

Opening Hours
Banks are generally open Monday to Friday, 8.30 a.m. to 4 or 4.30 p.m.

Post offices, as a rule, open Monday to Friday 8 a.m to 5 p.m. and Saturday morning 8 a.m. to noon.

There are no set hours for shops, though they tend to open daily and keep long hours.

Government offices open from around 8 a.m. to noon and 1 p.m. to 5 p.m.

Temples and monasteries keep more restricted hours, and it's best to get to them in the morning to be sure to find them open.

Photography
Vientiane and Luang Prabang are the best places for buying film. Developing in Laos can be fairly expensive, and it might be better to wait till you've moved on. Remember that the tropical light is at its best for a couple of hours after sunrise and just before sunset, and very harsh from midmorning to mid-afternoon. Make sure you keep your film in a cool place and out of the sun. When taking people's photographs, ask for their permission first.

Public Transport
Because of the mountainous terrain and poor roads, travelling overland through Laos is both scenically beautiful and painfully slow. Add to this the rickety nature of the inter-city buses, the uncomfortable seats and the heat, and it can be just painful. The journey time between Vientiane and Luang Prabang, for example, is approximately 10 hours. Still, it's the cheapest way of getting around, and many will argue that it's the best way to see the country—but you will need to spend plenty of time in Laos for this option to be viable.

Given that the country is dominated by the mighty Mekong River and its many tributaries, it's no surprise that the traditional method of transport is by boat. You can travel between the main cities on the Mekong by slow boat (Vientiane-Luang Prabang takes about 5 days) or cruise ships. Less traditional are the incredibly noisy powerboats that cover the distances quickly, but are cramped and uncomfortable.

If you're pressed for time, you'll probably find yourself taking to the air. Lao Aviation is the only airline operating internal flights in Laos, and flies to most of the larger regional cities. It doesn't have the best reputation among the world's airlines— some foreign embassies advise their staff not to fly on it—but there are now some decent newer planes such as the ATR 72 in the fleet.

In town, the most practical and inexpensive way to get around is by the brightly painted, three-wheel motorcycle taxi known as a Jumbo. This is very much a home-grown product, where a basic carriage is soldered onto a motorbike that has been cut in two. The more famous *tuk-tuk* is the Japanese-made version, popular throughout South-East Asia. The cyclo, or cycle-rickshaw, is a slower, but more traditional mode of transport, and rarely sighted these days. There are some taxi cars available, especially at the airports. If you prefer to use one of these at other times, ask your hotel desk to arrange one for you. Whichever type of taxi you take, though, always agree on the price in advance

Safety

Laos is generally safe for tourists, and its citizens are rarely anything other than friendly and courteous to visitors. But it's also a very poor country, and it's worthwhile taking some basic safety precautions, especially in Vientiane. Make sure valuables are kept in the hotel safe. Carry your passport, cash and travellers cheques in a money belt or seal-able pocket, and be especially vigilant in crowded places where pickpockets operate, such as busy tourist sites. Be careful not to stray too far off the beaten track alone at night. If you're heading out into the remoter countryside, check first that the roads are free of bandit activity, and also take extreme caution when walking off main paths: there is still a vast amount of unexploded ordnance left over from the Vietnam War.

Time

Standard time in Laos is GMT+7.

Tipping

Tipping isn't customary in Laos. But bear in mind that wages are extremely low, and it wouldn't be considered amiss to leave a small tip in hotels and restaurants, at your discretion.

Toilets

Public toilets will be a rare sight on your travels around the country, so whenever you're in tourist-friendly places such as cafés, restaurants, hotels and museums remember to make use of the facilities before leaving.

Voltage

Electric current is generally 220V, 50 cycle A.C. Power cuts are not infrequent, although most of the larger hotels now have back-up generators. Bring a torch just in case.

INDEX

Airports 98
Baci 94
Ban Saphai 93
Ban That 92
Bolovens Plateau
    93–94
Champasak
    Province 92–94
Climate 98
Communications 98
Dining out 96–97
Driving 99
Emergencies 99
Festivals 100–101
Formalities 99
Health 99
History 77–80
Holidays 100–101
Khon Phapheng
    Falls 94
Kouang Si
    Waterfall 91
Language 101
Luang Prabang
    87–90
    Chinatown 88–89
    Lower Town 90
    Mekong 90
    Old City 87–90
    Phu Si 89
    Royal Palace 87–88
    Wat Aham 89
    Wat Mai 88
    Wat Pakkhan 90
    Wat Wisunalat 89
    Wat Xiang Thong
        89–90
Media 101

Money matters
    101–102
Opening Hours 102
Pak Ou Caves 91
Pakse 92–93
Photography 102
Plain of Jars 91
Public transport
    102–103
Safety 103
Savannakhet 92
Shopping 95
Suan Vathanatham 86
Time 103
Tipping 103
Toilets 103
Vang Vieng 86
Vientiane 81–84
    City centre 81–84
    Colonial Quarter 82
    Lan Xang
    Avenue 84–85
    Lao National
    Museum 82
    Mekong River 84
    Nam Phou Place 82
    Patuxai Arch 85
    Presidential
    Palace 82
    That Luang 85–86
    Wat Haw Phra
    Kaew 82–83
    Wat Ong Teu 84
    Wat Si Muang 84
    Wat Si Saket 83–84
Voltage 103
Wat Phu 94
Wat Xieng Khuan 86

104

GENERAL EDITOR
    Barbara Ender-Jones
LAYOUT
    André Misteli
PHOTO CREDITS
    Renata Holzbachová:
    pp. 1, 4, 13, 16, 15;
    Hémisphères/Morandi: p. 20;
    Hémisphères/Gardel: p. 3
MAPS
    Elsner & Schichor;
    JPM Publications

Copyright © 2005, 2002
by JPM Publications S.A.
12, avenue William-Fraisse,
1006 Lausanne, Switzerland
E-mail:
information@jpmguides.com
Web site:
http://www.jpmguides.com/

Printed in Switzerland
Weber/Bienne (CTP) — 04/10/01
Edition 2005

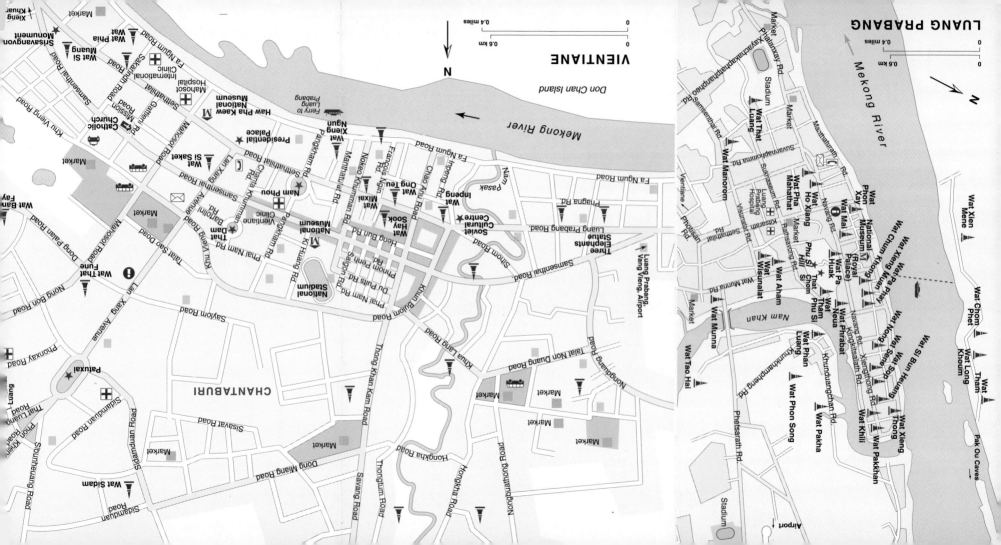

CAMBODIA

Dan Colwell

JPMGUIDES

This Way Cambodia

Land of the Khmers

Mention the word Cambodia, and it immediately conjures up idyllic images of intricate monumental art, graceful classical dancers and conical-hatted peasants hoeing in rice fields—but also nightmares of cruelty and suffering, and the ruthless destruction of a proud cultural heritage. Who could have imagined back in the 1960s the disastrous path Cambodia was about to embark upon? At that time, the kingdom of Cambodia, also called Srok Khmer, Land of the Khmers, was inhabited by a healthy, essentially rural population. Having recently emerged from French colonial rule, they appeared to live a tranquil and pacific life under the leadership of Prince Sihanouk, who was nudging the country forward towards the modern world.

But after 1970, the kingdom was thrown into chaos: first came the deposition of the prince and the declaration of a republic. Then Cambodia felt the full, terrible effect of the Vietnam War (1970–75). This culminated in the ordeal of four years under the totalitarian Khmer Rouge regime headed by the infamous Pol Pot, when the people were transformed into slaves of the state and the cultural patrimony of the nation systematically eradicated. There was no escaping this madness—which resulted in the deaths of more than a million citizens by massacre, starvation and disease—except by paying the price of foreign occupation. In 1979, disaffected Khmer troops backed by the Vietnamese Army invaded Cambodia and overthrew the Pol Pot government.

A Hopeful Future

Little by little, Cambodia has striven to heal its wounds and to open the door to the future. In the last few years the reconstruction of the nation's political, economic and cultural life has gathered pace. For a start, the monarchy—the symbolic and aesthetic core of its equilibrium—has been restored. Parts of Cambodia such as the areas north and west of Siem Reap, which were closed off until the late 1990s due to the threat of banditry by remnants of the Khmer Rouge, are now open for travel. A fast, comfortable highway has been built to link Phnom Penh with the coastal resort of Sihanoukville, and work has begun on upgrading the road to Siem Reap and the temples at Angkor.

Phnom Penh is once again a busy South-East Asian capital. Tourists are returning to one of the world's greatest sights, the remarkable medieval city of Angkor. The nearby town of Siem Reap is undergoing something of a boom as a result, with a flurry of hotel-building taking place.

Carnival on Water

Demonstrating a welcome continuity with the past, the lives of the 13.3 million inhabitants, 96 per cent of ethnic Khmer stock, remain closely tied to the ebb and flow of the Mekong River. The capital, Phnom Penh, rises at the junction of the Mekong and one of its tributaries, the Tonlé Sap, whose waters feed into a small lake on the north side of town. This tributary is unusual in that it reverses its flow twice a year. From October to June, it flows from the northwest to the southeast, but at the beginning of June, the pressure of the Mekong, then starting to flood, is so great that it manages to push back the Tonlé Sap, causing it to run upstream and spill into the great lake of the same name in the centre of the country, thus increasing its depth five-fold. The sea-

sonal inversion of the waters in late October is the occasion of a grand spectacle in Phnom Penh, the Water Festival, featuring colourful canoe races. In the old days, the king would order a royal monk to cut a rope stretched across the river, thus "liberating" the waters and reversing the current. Modern Cambodians use it as an excuse to pour into the capital and enjoy the carnival atmosphere, and to celebrate the sheer marvel of the nation's survival.

Few could claim that travel here is easy—the roads generally have more potholes than flat surfaces, and facilities outside the main cities often leave a lot to be desired. But wherever you go in Cambodia, your way will be smoothed along by its fascinating landscape, the grandeur of its monuments, the charm and friendliness of its handsome, resilient people.

107

Flashback

Early History

Neolithic peoples were living in Cambodia from around 4000 BC, though it's not known where they originally came from. Archaeological evidence suggests they lived in houses built on wooden piles and ate mainly fish, practices strikingly similar to those of rural Cambodians today.

From the 1st century AD, the culture took on a decided Indian cast, mainly due to the establishment of trade links between South-East Asia and the sub-continent. By the 3rd century AD a Sanskrit-style alphabet was in place, along with Indian-influenced arts and religion. Indeed, Hinduism would exist alongside Buddhism as a central aspect of Khmer culture for the next 1,000 years. At this time a Hindu-Buddhist kingdom arose in southern Cambodia and Vietnam; the Chinese—the only source of information on the period—knew it as Funan. On the Mekong delta, the kingdom became a powerful maritime empire and expanded over the entire Indochinese peninsula.

The gigantic carved heads of Angkor Thom's Bayon face the four points of the compass.

Funan began to decline during the 6th century. Chinese writers refer to two successor kingdoms in the region: Water Chenla, which occupied the delta, and Land Chenla, based further up the Mekong in northern Cambodia and southern Laos. Over the next three centuries, these seem to have fragmented even further into several small kingdoms. Politically divided, the region became prey to attacks from the expansionist Srivijaya empire in Sumatra. And yet from this dangerously vulnerable position, Khmer culture was about to enter its golden age.

Angkor Period

In 790 a young prince from Java, who claimed Cambodian descent, gained a foothold in the eastern part of the country. By 802 he had established his capital in the north of Cambodia, not far from where Angkor was later built, and was consecrated as a *chakravatin* (an Indian concept of "world ruler") under the name of Jayavarman II. Vital in creating a unified, centralized state, his reign ushered in the long and glorious era of classical Khmer civilization. Soon after his death, the capital was moved to Roluos, just north of the Tonlé Sap lake. Here, his successor Indravarman I built the first of the great Khmer monuments, including the Bakong, a temple-mountain which served as a model for many of the subsequent royal temples at Angkor.

Indravarman's son, Yasovarman I (reigned 889–910), shifted the capital to Angkor. Relying on an agrarian economy with increasingly sophisticated methods of irrigation, Angkor developed into the foremost regional power, taking control of the Mekong Valley and central Vietnam, and pushing its empire into present-day Laos and Thailand. Several of its rulers used the wealth and manpower of the nation to build magnificent palaces and temples. However, the draining effect this had on the society was partly responsible for some of its subsequent difficulties. Angkor was subject to periodic bouts of disorder and warfare during the 10th and 11th centuries, and faced disintegration as rival contenders fought for the throne.

The rise of a new dynasty in the 12th century ensured a last flowering of Khmer culture. With the accession of Suryavarman II in 1113, Angkor once again had a mighty warrior-king on the throne. He led a celebrated campaign against the Champa kingdom of Vietnam but is best known today as the builder of Angkor Wat. There was one more great king to come. In 1177 Jayavarman VII pacified the traditional enemies from Champa, and to further protect the state had the huge city of Angkor Thom constructed, with the extraordinary Bayon temple at its centre. But the state had already begun to pass its peak. At the death of Jayavarman VII, in around 1219, Angkor had reached the beginning of the end.

Fall of Angkor

The decline turned out to be long and gradual. But eventually the arrival of more dynamic Indochinese empires, coupled with a transformation in the structure of the state—the hierarchical Hindu concept of god-king was replaced by Theravada Buddhism—took their toll. Repeated attacks on Angkor in the 14th and 15th centuries by the Thai kingdom based at Ayutthaya devastated Khmer power. The city was sacked in 1431, after which Angkor was abandoned and a new capital founded at the confluence of the Mekong and the Tonlé Sap, near present-day Phnom Penh. Apart from a brief resurgence in the mid-16th century, when they recaptured Angkor, the Khmers underwent a series of weak monarchs and bad defeats, becoming in effect a vassal state of their two neighbours.

In 1794 the Thais appropriated Angkor and the western provinces of Cambodia. To the east, the Vietnamese seized the Mekong delta and the Khmer port of Prey Nokor, the future Saigon.

French Rule

During the 19th century Cambodia's kings relied more and more on foreign support, in effect becoming pawns in a regional power struggle between the Thais and Vietnamese. By the middle of the century the country was facing the threat of being completely swallowed up by its neighbours, and so when King Norodom signed a treaty with France in 1863 turning Cambodia into a French protectorate, one of its results was to guarantee the survival of the Cambodian state. The French administered the country, deciding in effect who would be on the throne and how the country would be run. Meanwhile, French archaeologists began excavations at Angkor, bringing it to the attention of the outside world; and in 1907 it was finally returned to Cambodian control by the Thais.

French colonial rule was temporarily ended by the Japanese in World War II, at which time the 18-year-old Prince Sihanouk acceded to the throne. The French regained power in 1945, but eight years later Cambodia achieved full independence. Sihanouk had been instrumental in the negotiations with the French, and in 1954 his government was recognized as the legitimate authority in the nation.

Cambodia and the Vietnam War

Though Sihanouk followed a policy of neutrality in relation to the war raging in Vietnam, his suspicion of American intentions in the region meant that he was broadly sympathetic to the North Vietnamese communists. As a result, in 1970 the pro-American General Lon Nol overthrew Sihanouk and launched an attack on North Vietnamese troops stationed inside the eastern border of the country. This proved a disastrous move on two counts. The Cambodian army, no match for the battle-hardened Vietnamese, was easily defeated, and it had the effect of involving Cambodia in the Vietnam War. Even worse, when the Vietnam War officially ended after the Paris cease-fire agreement in 1973, the Cambodian communists (the Khmer Rouge) refused to adhere to it. In response, the Americans carried out massive aerial bombardments of Cambodia, despite there being no state of war between the countries. In fact, the US dropped more bombs on the country than it had on Japan during the whole of World War II. Paradoxically, the main result of the havoc wreaked by this was to hasten the collapse of the Lon Nol government. In April 1975, Khmer Rouge troops entered Phnom Penh, opening a new and terrible chapter of Cambodian history.

Khmer Rouge in Power

Under the leadership of Saloth Sar, a former teacher better known as Pol Pot, and influenced by the Cultural Revolution in Mao's China, the Khmer Rouge set about establishing a totally collectivized state, where the entire population was forced to work the land in the effort to increase rice production. Phnom Penh and other towns were emptied; people suspected of being from the educated middle class were systematically murdered, while many more died from overwork, starvation and disease. The country was effectively cut off from the rest of the world for the next four years.

In 1979, the regime's belligerence towards Vietnam prompted a military invasion that swept aside the army and caused the Khmer Rouge leadership to flee to Thailand. During their short time in power, the Khmer Rouge had been responsible for the deaths of around 1 million Cambodians—15 per cent of the total population.

Cambodia Today

Under the political influence of Vietnam, Cambodia returned to something approaching normality. Private property was re-introduced and the practice of Buddhism permitted; schools were re-opened and the cities repopulated. When the Vietnamese withdrew in 1989, the country was still left to face considerable problems, not least from continuing Khmer Rouge guerrilla activity in the north and west. And though Sihanouk was restored to the throne in 1993, the political scene remained extremely volatile. The 1997 elections saw his son, Prince Ranariddh, elected as prime minister, only to be ousted in a coup led by his co-incumbent, Hun Sen. New elections in 1998—the same year that Pol Pot died in the jungle out on the Thai border—confirmed Hun Sen's Cambodian People's Party in power.

Despite the bitter legacy of the recent past still haunting the nation—issues such as the arrest and trial of former Khmer Rouge leaders, the clearance of landmines, and a shattered economy continue to loom large—Cambodia has nonetheless entered the new millennium in a welcome state of peace and stability, with a rediscovered pride in its cultural heritage and renewed optimism about the future.

On the Scene

Cambodia has two main hubs for exploring the country. Phnom Penh, the capital, provides a perfect introduction to the culture, with its magnificent Royal Palace and fine museums. From the city centre, speedboats head northeast to Kratie, where there's a group of rare Irrawaddy river dolphins, while buses run to the laid-back beach resort of Sihanoukville, basking by the warm waters of the Gulf of Thailand. Almost every visitor will stay in Siem Reap at some point. This pleasant, easy-going little town is the base for trips to Cambodia's world renowned temples at Angkor. From here you will also find boats that go into the northwest of the country, where out-of-the-way towns such as Battambang retain their attractive colonial-era architecture.

▶ PHNOM PENH
Palace Quarter, Central Phnom Penh,
South of the City, Around Phnom Penh

With its bustling boulevards, riverside walks and fascinating mix of modern and traditional buildings, Phnom Penh is one of South-East Asia's most appealing cities. It was founded in 1434 after the Khmers had abandoned Angkor but remained something of a backwater until 1865, when King Norodom established it as his capital under the French Protectorate. During this period, the Royal Palace, National Museum and several colonial buildings were erected. The city was occupied by the Japanese in World War II, and in 1975 the entire population was evacuated by the Khmer Rouge. Throughout the city's traumatic recent history, the Royal Palace quarter remained the symbolic heart of the nation, and is the obvious place to begin your visit.

Palace Quarter
Ranged around the Royal Palace are monasteries, ministries, work-

shops and residences, forming respectively the monarchy's four pillars of religion, politics, art and family. Most of the buildings here date from the era of French rule, and as you wander around the leafy streets of the quarter it's tempting to see in their scale and grandeur a reflection of colonial, rather than royal, power.

Royal Palace

Located behind a protective wall topped with lotus-shaped crenellations, the Royal Palace has once more become the residence of King Sihanouk. It's composed of a number of small pavilions set in courtyards according to a specific layout, where material objects oppose things spiritual, and public faces private. At the end of the 19th century, the palace was a small city in itself with several thousand people bustling about. The majority of the buildings were pulled down for reconstruction in 1910.

Bestriding the wall, and facing the river, the Chan Chaya Pavilion was originally the impressive entrance to the palace and used for special performances of Khmer music and dance.

The Throne Hall is behind the pavilion and dominates the palace. Despite its modern materials, it's one of the most beautiful examples of Cambodian architecture, and deeply influenced by classical Khmer style. The splendid spire, 59 m (193 ft) high, has four sculpted faces similar to those on the Bayon at Angkor. The sumptuous interior is covered with murals depicting scenes from the *Ramayana*, and also contains the gilded coronation throne. Unfortunately, the general public is not allowed inside.

Not far from here is a marvellously anomalous French pavilion, given by Napoleon III to the Empress Eugénie and then passed on as a gift to King Norodom in 1876.

Reached via a gate just south of the pavilion, the Silver Pagoda was built from wood in 1892, then reconstructed in 1962. It's so named because the floor is paved with thousands of silver tiles weighing a kilogram apiece. The pagoda shelters a superb standing Buddha in gold that's adorned with more than 9,000 diamonds, the collective work of several jewellers at the beginning of the 20th century. There's also an exquisite seated Emerald Buddha dating from the 17th century.

In the courtyard outside, painted on the walls that enclose the pagoda, royal stupas, libraries, a pavilion containing a footprint of the Buddha, and an equestrian statue of King Norodom, is a fine set of traditional paintings illustrating the Cambodian *Ramayana*.

National Museum

Just north of the palace, the red-brick National Museum was built in pure Khmer style in 1917 by a French architect, with the help of the last traditional local architects. It houses a first-rate collection of Khmer art dating from the pre-Angkorian era through to the 20th century. The highlights are the sculptures, statues and other artefacts retrieved from Angkor, notably the red sandstone bas-relief from Banteay Srei and the sublime portrait head of Jayavarman VII, dating from the late 12th century. Throughout the country you'll see recreations of this image representing one of Angkor's greatest kings .

Central Phnom Penh

The distances covered in this section might be too great to accomplish entirely on foot, especially in very hot weather. So hop on the back of a *moto* to get from one place to another—the drivers are generally very good, and it's an entertaining way to see the city. But one spot made for walking is the Tonlé Sap riverside, where it seems as though all of Phnom Penh gathers each afternoon to enjoy the sunset.

Stunning decor at Wat Phnom, where worshippers flock to pray for good fortune.

Independence Monument

This huge monument occupies a traffic island south of the Palace Quarter at the corner of Norodom and Preah Sihanouk boulevards. Built in the shape of a lotus, it was completed in 1958 and celebrates Cambodia's independence from France, which took place five years earlier.

Sisowath Quay

Running north from the Royal Palace along the Tonlé Sap river, Sisowath Quay is lined with cafés and restaurants and is a constant hive of activity. You'll find early-morning joggers, late-afternoon strollers and at all times a bevy of fruit sellers and drink stalls. The views reach across to where the Tonlé Sap meets the Mekong. You can also take boats from here out onto the river.

Wat Ounalom

Set back from the Tonlé Sap to the north of the National Museum, this large temple complex is the headquarters of Cambodian Buddhism. It was founded in the 15th century, soon after the Khmers left Angkor. The temple's prominence in the religious life of the country meant that in the late 1970s it became the focus of Khmer Rouge aggression, when its chief priest was murdered and the important library of Buddhist texts destroyed.

Central Market

Away from the river, the busy streets in the centre of town converge on the striking yellow façade of the huge Art Deco Psah Thmei. Built by the French in 1937 with a dome and four radiating wings, it houses a marvellous range of stalls selling everything from jewellery to toasted spiders, and should be visited by anyone wanting colourful photos of Cambodian life.

Wat Phnom

To the north of the city centre, Wat Phnom is situated on a hill 27 m (88 ft) high ("Phnom" means hill in Khmer). Legend has it that in 1372, a woman named Penh discovered four statues of the Buddha on the nearby riverbank and placed them in a purpose-built pagoda on the hill. The settlement that grew up around it acquired the name Phnom Penh, the hill of Penh. There's a small statue of Madame Penh in the pavilion next to the large stupa containing the ashes of King Ponhea Yat, who died in 1467 and was the Angkorian king responsible for establishing Phnom Penh as the nation's main city after the abandonment of Angkor.

The temple can be reached via a superb staircase guarded by terracotta lions and two vast nagas—mythical, multi-headed snakes.

Colonial Quarter

The former French end of town stretches around Wat Phnom and continues northwards. Here there remain some fine colonial houses, the administrative offices of the old protectorate (including various public buildings in colonial style), the Descartes School, the Calmette Hospital and the French Embassy, both on Monivong Boulevard, and the Bibliothèque Nationale. This is next to the famous Hotel Le Royal, which opened in 1929. Following years of neglect after the rise of the Khmer Rouge, it has now been restored to its former splendour. Finally, you can check out the small, delightfully old-fashioned French residential area centred around Street 47, once known appropriately enough as Rue de France.

South of the City

The area south of central Phnom Penh is home to the well-known Psah Tuol Tum Pong, also called the Russian Market, which attracts many visitors as well as locals. But overshadowing everything else are two emotionally charged sites that recall the dark days of the Pol Pot regime.

Tuol Sleng Museum

Located in the former Tuol Svay Prey High School only a kilometre or so from the city centre, this is also known as the Genocide Museum. It's never less than a grim experience, but perhaps also a vital one for any understanding of modern Cambodian history. During the Khmer Rouge regime, the school was run by a secret department code-named S-21; it served as a centre of interrogation and torture for people of all ages and social ranks. At least 14,000 perished, though the figure is probably higher. Almost unbearably harrowing photographs, paintings, eye-witness accounts and other documents testify to the murderous insanity that gripped the country's leadership and its functionaries at the time, and the terrible price that its citizens had to pay.

Killing Fields of Choeung Ek

The victims of Tuol Sleng's torture cells were brought to these fields 15 km (9 miles) south of the city, where they were usually bludgeoned to death to avoid the cost of using bullets. After the Pol Pot regime was defeated by the Vietnamese army in 1979, the mass graves found here contained the remains of 8,985 people. It's now a peaceful, solemn place, and the glass memorial stupa filled with the skulls of those found nearby makes a powerfully emotive centrepiece. In front of it are the craters left by the excavated graves.

117

Around Phnom Penh

Beyond the city are several interesting sites, including the remains of a couple of Angkor-era cities. They also offer the chance to enjoy a taste of rural Cambodia.

Mekong Island

Boats leave from near Wat Ounalom for day trips to this island in the river north of Phnom Penh. On the island you can ride on an elephant, see silk being woven, and enjoy classical Khmer dancing. The island's residents are mainly boat fishermen—look out for an unusual boat temple.

Udong

About 35 km (22 miles) to the north, Udong is situated on the hilly ridge of Preah Reach Throap. It became the capital of Cambodia in 1618 after one of Phnom Penh's many periods of abandonment, and remained the royal stronghold until King Norodom re-established the capital at Phnom Penh in 1865. It once boasted hundreds of buildings, temples and royal stupas, but most of these were destroyed in the early 1970s when Lon Nol ordered air strikes against Khmer Rouge fighters based here. A few monasteries have survived, along with the funerary stupas of some of the last kings. Best of all, perhaps, is simply the sense of being away from the hustle and bustle of the city, something enhanced by the superb views of the surrounding countryside. For this reason, it has become a popular place for weekend picnickers.

Tonlé Bati

On the banks of the Tonlé Bati river, 33 km (20 miles) south of the capital, is the temple of Ta Prohm, built in the 12th century by Jayavarman VII. Made from laterite, decorated with bas-reliefs and sculptures, and with a layout similar to Angkor's grand temples, it gives a good idea of the essence of classical Khmer architecture if you are unable to get to Angkor itself. Be sure also to visit the nearby, smaller Yeay Peau temple. The area is another popular haunt with weekend day-trippers from Phnom Penh, who come to cool off by the river or float on one of the swan-shaped pleasure boats.

Phnom Chisor

These 11th-century hilltop ruins are located a further 20 km (12 miles) to the south from Tonlé Bati. The main temple, dedicated to Brahma, took a pounding from Lon Nol's troops and bombers in the early 1970s but still has some fine features, such as the carved sandstone lintels. Further compensation comes from the spectacular views of the countryside and the Tonlé Om lake.

THE ANGKOR SITES

Angkor Wat, Angkor Thom, Around Angkor,
Roluos Group, Banteay Srei

The Angkor temples are the vestiges of religious constructions in stone from a dozen different Khmer capitals and their satellite cities. Built and rebuilt between the 9th and 16th centuries, the ensemble comprises a thousand monuments spread over as many square kilometres. Some are reduced to rubble, impossible to identify. For technical and ritualistic reasons, the most spectacular, such as Angkor Wat and the Bayon, were built between the 10th and 13th centuries and are mainly concentrated in an area of 50 sq km (19 sq miles) north of Siem Reap. This cluster is Angkor proper, though its true name is Yashodharapura, as Angkor merely means "city".

It's probable that when you're not at Angkor, you'll be in Siem Reap. This pleasant town is where the hotels, restaurants and cafés are located. You can also take an excursion from here to the Tonlé Sap lake and its fascinating Vietnamese Floating Village.

Angkor Wat

Protected by a massive moat and outer walls, and reached by a long causeway, the temple-mountain of Angkor Wat is undoubtedly the greatest masterpiece of Khmer architecture. In recent times its five mighty towers have become the symbol of the Cambodian people's cultural pride and identity. Unlike most of the buildings at Angkor, it seems to have been in continual use by Buddhist monks since the area was abandoned in the 15th century. However, when the temple was built in the first half of the 12th century under King Suryavarman II, it was dedicated to the Hindu god Vishnu. It's the only temple to face west. This is probably because Vishnu was identified with the west, but also suggests that it was intended to be used as the king's mausoleum. It also means that the favoured time for visitors to come here now and climb up to the towers is sunset.

Make sure you leave enough time to pore over the magnificent bas-reliefs that stretch for 800 m (875 yd) around the wall of the temple. Packed with movement and a thrilling sense of drama, they depict scenes from the Hindu epics, the *Mahabarata* and the *Ramayana*, as well as events from the reign of Suryavarman II. Look out, too, for the evocative Heaven and Hell gallery, and the splendid Churning of the Ocean of Milk, where two great teams of gods and devils play tug-of-war using a serpent to see who will win immortality.

Angkor Thom

Following the capture of Angkor in a surprise attack by the Chams in 1177, Jayavarman VII founded a new and final city not far from Angkor Wat. The colossal Angkor Thom was inspired by a new religious faith, a mystic Buddhism whose impressive hallmark is the four-faced Buddha. But tucked behind huge defensive laterite walls with their five great gates, the city was clearly built with a military purpose in mind.

Bayon

In the centre of Angkor Thom rises the breathtaking temple-mountain of the Bayon, where the distinction between architecture and sculpture disappears. Despite its ruined condition and the undoubted architectural problems caused when a third level was superimposed on the second,

---

A CIVILIZATION BUILT ON WATER

The monuments of Angkor were closely tied to a complex system of irrigation that made use of immense artificial reservoirs known as *barays*, and earned for the Khmer capital the name of "hydraulic city". In fact, building a successful city-state in Asia, where the monsoon rains are so unevenly distributed, necessarily involved stocking water to be shared out evenly over the course of the seasons, and thus ensuring a good, regular harvest. This hydraulic network was developed in a particularly genial location in the plain between the Phnom Koulen hills to the north and the fish-breeding Tonlé Sap lake to the south. The linchpin of the empire, the reservoir system became a genuine machine for intensive cereal production, assuring two or three crops per year—enough to supply the 1 million people who lived in the capital as workers, forced labourers and soldiers. But the over-exploitation of the fragile land, combined with deforestation, impoverished the earth, clogged up and dried out the hydraulic network. By the 14th century, the kings of Angkor were finding it hard to nourish their people, and in the face of intensifying attacks by the Thais, abandoned their monumental city. Declining economically, deprived of its political functions, deserted little by little by its "urban" population, Angkor largely returned to the forest, not to be cleared of the overgrowth of trees and foliage until archaeologists and tourists began arriving in the late 19th century.

Stern-faced gods line the causeways of Angkor Thom, leading from gates built with enough headroom for elephant and howdah to pass through.

cramping the courtyards and galleries, it retains an extraordinarily enigmatic and exotic power. The level of artistic creativity in evidence here is awesome, with richly carved bas-reliefs and a forest of towers showing the heads of Buddha that significantly resemble Jayavarman VII himself.

Baphuon

Currently undergoing restoration, the nearby Baphuon is part of an earlier city on this site. Built in the 11th century by King Udayadityavarman II, it's another temple-mountain and represents the mythical Mount Meru.

Royal Palace

To the north, in front of a vast square delineated by a row of twelve laterite towers, the royal palace has been reduced over time to its base. On the façade is the Terrace of the Elephants, with a marvellous bas-relief procession of tuskers. Just along from here, the statue of the Leper King on the terrace is a copy—the original is displayed in the National Museum in Phnom Penh. Archaeologists have still not determined whether it represents one of the Angkorian kings known to have suffered from leprosy. The raised platform itself was probably used for ceremonial cremations.

121

Around Angkor

Surrounding Angkor Wat and Angkor Thom are numerous ancient temples in varying states of repair. The best of them are on the main circuit and easily reached on relatively good roads.

Preah Khan

Just north of the city walls of Angkor Thom, the university-monastery of Preah Khan was consecrated in 1191 by Jayavarman VII in honour of his father. It's a vast complex with a maze of courtyards and corridors. In the northeastern part of the monastery, look out for a remarkable two-storey structure which, with its classical columns and carvings, might easily have been transported here from Ancient Rome.

Neak Pean

Not far from Preah Khan, the 12th-century Neak Pean temple was built in the middle of a pool. It has long been dry, though, which means that you're able to walk over to it and inspect the two intertwining nagas encircling the base of the temple, and the mysterious statue of a horse from which human legs protrude.

Banteay Kdei

The late-12th-century Banteay Kdei is a Buddhist temple with a real lost-city atmosphere, enhanced by the fact that fewer tourists tend to come to it. As you enter, a great sight of endlessly receding doorways draws you inside. Leave at the far end and you'll come to a raised stone platform with a superb view over the Srah Srang pond, which was possibly used as a pool for ritualized bathing.

Ta Prohm

Jayavarman VII was clearly a dutiful son, for the Ta Prohm monastery, just west of Banteay Kdei, this time commemorates his mother. Dating from 1186, it served as the administrative centre for the empire's 102 hospitals. Archaeologists made a deliberate decision to leave Ta Prohm as they found it, and so it offers a rare chance to see how Angkor looked when the first Europeans arrived in the 19th century. It's a breathtaking sight. With trees emerging out of temple buildings, and thick roots covering ruined passageways and courtyards, the jungle here has become part of the architecture.

Prasat Kravan

South of Banteay Kdei, the striking red-brick temples of Prasat Kravan are among the oldest in Angkor and date from 921. They were built as Hindu temples, and inside them are fine bas-reliefs of Vishnu and his consort, Lakshmi.

Phnom Bakheng

Take the trouble to climb Phnom Bakheng (though you can ride up on an elephant). The five-tiered temple mountain was founded during the reign of Yasovarman I and was the first of its kind to be built in Angkor. The best time to be here is at sunset, when the view over Angkor Wat and the western baray is stunning.

Roluos Group

The first true hydraulic Angkorian city, and the first significant monumental ensemble, was the city of Hariharalaya, built in the 9th century under Indravarman I. The city stretched to the south of the Baray of Lokei, or Indratataka, nearly 4 km (2.5 miles) long by 700 m (half a mile) wide. Better known as the Roluos group today, the surviving structures are located 15 km (9 miles) east of Siem Reap.

Taken together, they constitute the first great flowering of Khmer culture.

The heart of the city was the ancestral temple of Preah Ko, which housed the statues of the ancient king-protectors of the empire, and the magnificent temple-mountain of the Bakong. Built in 881, this was dedicated to the Hindu god, Shiva, and with its high central tower—a design that would reach its apogee in Angkor Wat—is a symbolic representation of Mount Meru.

Constructed on an island in the middle of the baray—which is now dry—the red-sandstone towers of Lolei temple were also intended for Hindu worship. They were consecrated to the memory of the founder of the city by his son, Yasovarman I. The portals of the temples are covered in Sanskrit writing and there are superb carvings around the entrances.

ANGKOR PROCEDURES

You'll need to arrange a taxi, moto or tour bus in order to get around the temples. The entire area is well organized and served by good roads. You can enter by buying a pass for 1, 2–3 or 4–7 days. A passport-sized photo is required, though you can have your photo taken on the spot if you've forgotten to bring one. The site is open from sunrise to sunset. There's a staggering amount of buildings worth seeing, and it would take a week to see most of them. However, the ones mentioned in this section comprise all the main temples in and around Angkor, and can be comfortably covered within 3 days.

Every part of Banteay Srei temple is exquisitely carved.

Banteay Srei

This small temple was built some 20 km (12 miles) upstream from Angkor during the 10th century. Here, the officiating Brahman would bless the water supplying the capital, fulfilling a symbolic role of guardian of the site and the dynasty. The temple was off-limits to visitors for many years because Khmer Rouge bandits were operating in the region, but it is now a safe and very popular side trip. It's distinguished by the colour—a glorious pink sandstone. A delightful entrance path leads to the three main pyramidal towers, with beautifully detailed carvings and ornamental work.

Kobal Spean

The famous River of a Thousand Lingas, 10 km (6 miles) further on, is a tranquil spot in which to view an intriguing array of 11th-century riverbed carvings.

Phnom Kulen

Not far from here is Cambodia's most sacred mountain. This is where in 802, Jayavarman II proclaimed himself the first god-king of Angkor. It's a tough, two-hour haul to the top, where you'll find a pagoda near a spring which is the source of the Tonlé Sap lake. Don't stray off the paths, as this area is still not completely clear of landmines.

Getting anywhere even slightly out of the way remains an arduous task. With poor road and rail communications, you can only reach places such as Kratie and Battambang by boat, or go further afield by internal flights. The delightful seaside resort of Sihanoukville is the glorious exception to the rule, with air-conditioned express buses rattling along to it from Phnom Penh on the American-built Highway 4 in just a few hours.

Sihanoukville

The town grew up around the port of Kampong Som on the Gulf of Thailand, which was itself established only in 1955 following Cambodian independence, as during colonial times the French had used Vietnam as their trading base in Indochina. There's not a lot to see here—the pleasure is all in discovering empty beaches, warm seas and a relaxed alternative to the relentlessly fast pace of the capital.

Lying just offshore are Koh Tang and Koh Rong, a couple of tranquil little islands to which you can take a boat. The waters around them are especially popular with divers. Koh Tang has an unusual claim to fame as the location of the last battle of the Vietnam War in 1975, when the US battled with Khmer Rouge troops here.

Ream National Park

When you've had enough of beachlife, try the wildlife. Nearby Ream National Park has been a protected area since 1993, and its unspoilt island-studded coastline is home to dolphins, monkeys, eagles and some beautiful coral in the sea.

Kratie

The Mekong has many marvels along its 4,350 km (2,700 miles), but the one that most delights visitors to Cambodia is near Kratie (pronounced "kra-chay"), an attractively sleepy little fishing town more than 300 km (186 miles) northeast of Phnom Penh. The river here is home to a colony of about 60 Irrawaddy dolphins. These snub-nosed, freshwater dolphins are increasingly rare. The best time to see them is during the dry season, when there's less water for them to hide in.

The road leading up to Kratie is the stuff of nightmares, but luckily you can take a boat from the capital along the Mekong, which should do the journey in a speedy 5 hours.

Battambang

Cambodia's second city is an attractive town with some of the country's finest colonial architecture. It's at the centre of Cambodia's rice-growing region; paddies dominate the landscape all the way to the Thai border. A walk along the River Sangker allows you to see many of the French shop houses once used by colonial traders, as well as enjoy the liveliest part of town—this area comes alive at night and is packed with food and drink stalls.

Battambang Museum

Near the river, the museum contains a collection of items from the region's temples, many of which date from the Angkor period. South of here, the former Governor's House is arguably the most splendid colonial building in the country.

Wat Banan

Located on a small hilltop 20 km (12 miles) south of the town is the 10th-century Wat Banan temple. With five laterite and sandstone towers, it conjures up something of the flavour of Angor Wat.

Phnom Sampau

About the same distance southwest of Battambang, Phnom Sampeau is a spectacular outcrop whose 600 steps will test your energy reserves to the limit. You'll find a temple on the top, as well as a couple of large field guns—this was an outpost of the Phnom Penh government's battle against Khmer Rouge rebels until late 1996.

Shopping

A shopping trip to one of the busy markets in Phnom Penh or Siem Reap is undoubtedly one of the most entertaining experiences Cambodia has to offer. Here, the everyday process of buying and selling becomes a full-blooded participation sport.

Psah Thmei, the vast Central Market in Phnom Penh, is packed with stalls selling cut gems and gold and silver items, as well as everything from souvenir T-shirts to mosquito nets. In the south of the city, Psah Tuol Tumpung, also known as the Russian Market, is a good place for made-to-measure clothes, silk and jewellery. The Old Market in Siem Reap has as many Angkor-influenced sculptures as you could want, as well as a good selection of books about Angkor and Cambodia in general. Fine copies of Angkorian bronzes are sometimes found on sale in the National Museum shop in Phnom Penh, cast according to traditional methods by old masters. You might also consider buying souvenir and handicraft items made by disabled victims of Cambodia's landmines. These can be found in shops set up by NGOs in the main cities.

Handwoven silk is first-rate. Silk is sold by the length—suffi-cient for a Khmer man's *sarong* or woman's flowery *sampot* (skirt). If you take a close look at any of the female statues in the museums, you'll see they are all wearing *sampots*. The plaid-like fabrics are reserved for men. There are also solid-colour lengths, sometimes with moiré effect. But look out for other items made from silk, such as bags and purses. Outside the city, you might like to buy a traditional scarf known as a *krama*. Made from silk or cotton, it's used by locals to keep the sun off their heads and dust out of their eyes.

Cambodian artisans were famous throughout the region for their skills. They were almost entirely wiped out under the Khmer Rouge, but some survived to keep the tradition going, and today there is a considerable amount of finely worked jewellery and silverware to be found. Be careful if you want to buy gold: it's often just plated. The norm is 24-carat.

Dining Out

Khmer cuisine has a long tradition of excellence dating back to the time when it was considered one of the fine arts of the royal court. At its best, it can hold its own with the more famous neighbouring cuisine of Thailand and Vietnam. Using aromatic herbs such as lemongrass, tamarind, coriander and mint, seasoned with a complex multitude of spices, it provides a delicious way of discovering an essential aspect of Cambodian culture.

You can sample Khmer cooking in a variety of different establishments, ranging from one of the small food stalls in the market to an elegant restaurant in downtown Phnom Penh. You'll also find any amount of good, inexpensive cooking from around the region, in particular Chinese and Thai food. What's more, old ties with the former colonial ruler haven't completely dissolved, and along with a healthy supply of baguettes and croissants, the main towns boast some first-rate French and other European restaurants.

Main Courses

Freshwater fish features heavily in Khmer cuisine, courtesy of the vast amount produced in the great Tonlé Sap lake and the Mekong River. Seafood comes from the coast on the Gulf of Thailand.

One of the great specialities of the country is *trei ang*, grilled fish which is usually dipped in *teuk trei*, a fish sauce used to salt food. Other mouthwatering fish dishes include *trei chorm hoi*, steamed whole fish, *trei neung phkea*, served with shrimps, and *trei chean neung spei*, fried with vegetables. Be sure to try *amok*, a delicious preparation of poached fish in a rich coconut sauce. You may also be curious to taste the more rustic dried (*nhiet*) or smoked (*ch'aeu*) fish, fermented fish dishes (*prahok*, *nam*) or the delectable prawns (*kapik*).

As for salads, *phlie sack ko* is composed of vegetables and herbs mixed with beef marinated in lemon juice; *ngom mon* is a chicken salad, *ngom trei* is the fish version. Also recommended is *khao phoun*, rice noodles in a coconut sauce.

Bananas and pineapple are incorporated into many savoury dishes.

Most dishes are accompanied by *samlo*, a substantial soup. *Samlo matiou banle* is a piquant fish-based soup with a slightly sour flavour, while spicy *samlo matiou bangkang* has prawns as the main ingredient. The tasty *samlo kroeung* resembles a meat stew. Look out also for *samlo chapek*, with pork and ginger, and *samlo ktis*, a fish soup sweetened with coconut and pineapple.

Sugary treats (*bangaem*) are usually reserved for festival days or religious offerings. However, if you like to finish off your meals on a sweet note, you'll find all sorts of pastries (*noum*), as well as jackfruit pudding (*sankcha khnor*) and little eggy cakes that are sold at street stalls.

Drinks

Tea and coffee are always available—the coffee may well come with condensed milk. Fresh fruit drinks (*tikaloks*) are made at street stalls; if you prefer them unsweetened say so, or they'll have plenty of sugar added. Co-conut juice is refreshingly cool and opened before your eyes.

Many of the restaurants in Phnom Penh and Siem Reap have surprisingly extensive wine lists. Cambodian beer such as Angkor is excellent, and goes well with spicy food.

129

The Hard Facts

Airports

Pochentong Airport is situated 8 km (5 miles) west of Phnom Penh; Siem Reap airport is 7 km (4 miles) outside town and serves tourists wanting to visit Angkor.

The terminals have fairly limited tourist information services, cafés, currency exchange and duty-free facilities. If you do not already have special arrangements made for the journey into town (some hotels offer a free pick-up service, for example), you'll find plenty of taxi drivers outside the terminal clamouring for your custom. If you don't want to haggle over price, you can buy a pre-paid voucher before leaving the building.

Note that Cambodia levies a departure tax on international and domestic flights from Pochentong and Siem Reap.

Climate

Cambodia has a tropical climate, with a southwest monsoon bringing heavy rains between May and October and a dry season that extends from November to April. The coolest month of the year is January when the daily average temperature is 28°C (82.4°F); the hottest is April, with temperatures reaching 40°C (104°F). In Sep-

tember and October, during the wettest months of the monsoon, roads can become impassable, and travel around the country might be difficult.

Communications

The postal service in Cambodia is relatively efficient, which is probably due to the fact that mail is sent first to Bangkok, where it then becomes part of the tried and trusted Thai airmail system. Along with selling stamps and phonecards, main post offices offer telephone, fax, e-mail and poste restante facilities. The main post office in Phnom Penh is on Phlauv 13, not far from Wat Phnom; at Siem Reap it's on the west side of the river south of the Grand Hotel d'Angkor.

International telephone calls are expensive. They are cheaper if made at the post office rather than from your hotel, and there's a significant reduction for calls made at the weekend. Camintel and Mobitel phonecards can be purchased from shops and hotels as well as the post office, and used in any of the numerous public phone booths found in the cities.

To call overseas from Cambo-dia, dial 001 + country code +

area code (minus the initial 0) + local number. The country code for Cambodia if you are dialling from abroad is 855; the city code for Phnom Penh is 023, Siem Reap 063, Sihanoukville 034.

Faxes can be sent and received at hotels, but are also expensive. The internet is very popular in Cambodia, and it's by far the cheapest way of regularly keeping in touch with people at home. There are plenty of Internet cafés, and larger hotels and post offices also offer this facility.

Driving

It is possible for foreign tourists to hire a car in Cambodia. However, there are compelling reasons not to do so. Apart from Highway 4 from Phnom Penh to Sihanoukville and Highway 7 as far as Kompong Cham, the condition of the roads is uniformly terrible, on top of which are the inevitable difficulties of driving in a country where no one seems to adhere to any kind of motoring rules. Car hire in Cambodia, therefore, mainly means hiring a car with a driver. Arranged through your hotel or a reputable travel agent, this can be a relatively stress-free option. You could also hire a motorbike. A bike provides independence and flexibility when looking around Angkor, for example, but you need to weigh up very carefully the dangers of travelling on unfamiliar Cambodian roads and through crowded city streets.

Emergencies

Emergency phone numbers:
    police: 117
    fire: 118
    ambulance: 119
For a police line where English and French are certain to be spoken dial 023 724 793. However, most problems can be handled at your hotel desk.

The emergency service of the European Dental Clinic is on 023 362 656; serious medical problems will probably entail evacuation to Bangkok—the International SOS Medical Centre can arrange these on 023 216 911.

Formalities

You will need a passport, valid for at least six months after your date of arrival. One-month tourist visas are issued on arrival and cost US$20.

Remember to bring a passport-size photo of yourself (and you'll need another for your Angkor pass). Should you forget, the officials at Pochentong Airport have a camera at the ready but will charge you for the service.

Health

Before you leave be sure to buy travel insurance that includes medical cover and have all necessary immunizations—contact your doctor or travel centre to find out what's required. You'll also need to start taking a course of antimalarial tablets prior to departure. Preventing the insects getting to you is best, though, so it's a good idea to take mosquito repellent cream, and keep arms and legs covered in the evenings if possible.

With a little care you should encounter no health problems during your stay. It's wise to avoid too much exposure to the sun. Wear a hat, use a good sunscreen and keep in the shade as much as possible, especially in the middle of the day. Drink plenty of mineral water to avoid dehydration—but never drink tap water. In the same vein, try to avoid salad and fruit that's been washed in unpurified water, ice cubes and fruit juice diluted with tap water—and brush your teeth in mineral water.

If you require specialized prescription medicines, remember to take enough with you to last for the duration of your stay in Cambodia.

Holidays and festivals

Many of Cambodia's public holidays and festivals follow the lunar calendar, and so move from year to year. During all of the following holidays, you'll find banks and offices shut, and at Cambodian New Year virtually the entire country is on the move, with most of the population seeming to head for the temples at Angkor:

January 1	New Year's Day
March 8	International Women's Day
May 1	Labour Day
June 1	International Children's Day
September 24	Constitution Day
October 23	Peace Day
Oct 30–Nov 1	King's Birthday
November 9	Independence Day
December 10	International Human Rights' Day

Moveable festivals:
Mid-April: *Bonn Chaul Chnam* (Cambodian New Year)
April/May: *Visaka Bochea* (Buddha's Birthday)
April/May: *Bonn Chrott Preah Nongkoal* (Royal Ploughing Festival)
Sept/Oct: *Pchum Ben* (Spirits Commemoration Festival)
November: *Bonn Om Touk* (Water and Moon Festival)—a major festival marking the reverse flow of the Tonlé Sap at the start of the dry season.

Language

The majority of Cambodians speak Khmer, a non-tonal language which theoretically makes it easier for Westerners to speak.

English is widely understood, especially by younger people, while French might still come in useful with older Cambodians.

Media

There are plenty of locally published English-language papers and magazines to choose from. The *Cambodia Daily* covers both national and international news and has a useful What's On section on Friday. The fortnightly *Phnom Penh Post* provides a well-written overview of Cambodian news and local interest stories, while *Vibe, The Cambodian Scene* is a glossy magazine dedicated to Cambodian lifestyle issues.

International newspapers such as *The Bangkok Post*, *International Herald Tribune*, and *Far Eastern Economic Review* can be found in Phnom Penh and Siem Reap.

Most medium- and top-range hotels have satellite TV, showing BBC, CNN, French and Japanese channels.

Short-wave radio enthusiasts can listen to BBC World Service, Voice of America and Radio Australia. The BBC World Service is also broadcast locally on 100FM radio.

Money matters

The unit of currency in Cambodia is the *riel*, issued in banknotes from 100 to 100,000, though notes above 10,000 riel are rarely sighted. There are no coins.

In recent years the riel has suffered from the effects of high inflation, and you'll find that the US dollar is not only used as the benchmark for prices, but also as a day-to-day part of the Cambodian monetary system, accepted by taxi drivers and shopkeepers alike. In the north of the country, Thai *baht* are also generally accepted.

Given that this is almost completely a cash economy with credit cards taken at only the most expensive hotels and restaurants (though even this is changing, and banks such as Mekong Bank have recently launched their own Visa card), it makes sense to bring enough money in low denomination US dollar bills and US dollar travellers cheques to cover such things as meals, travel and shopping for the duration of your holiday. You can obtain cash advances on credit cards at banks in Phnom Penh and Siem Reap, but doing so will incur heavy charges.

If you do bring other currencies, make sure you don't change too much into riels at any one time: it is not a convertible currency and banks and exchange bureaux won't buy back your unspent riels when you leave the country.

133

Opening hours

Banks are generally open from Monday to Friday from 8 a.m. to 3.30 p.m.

The main post offices in Phnom Penh and Siem Reap are open every day from 7 a.m. to 6 p.m. and 5 p.m. respectively.

There are no set hours for shops, though they tend to open daily, start early and close any time from early evening through till late.

Government offices and museums keep less demanding times, opening from around 8 a.m. to 11.30 a.m. and 2 p.m. to 5.30 p.m.

Photography

It's easy to buy film and have it developed at very reasonable prices in Phnom Penh and Siem Reap. Remember that the tropical light is at its best for a couple of hours after sunrise and just before sunset, and very harsh from mid-morning to mid-afternoon. Make sure you keep your film in a cool place and out of the sun.

When taking people's photographs, ask for their permission first.

Public Transport

Cambodia's public transport system is, to put it mildly, undeveloped. The limited train services to Battambang and Sihanoukville average a lamentable 20 kph (12 mph), and no-one but the most devoted train buff would even contemplate travelling on them.

Things aren't helped by the appalling state of the nation's roads. Although the country is fairly small, journeys by road are excruciatingly slow and uncomfortable. The exception to this is the excellent Highway 4 from Phnom Penh to the beach resort at Sihanoukville. A new sealed road between Phnom Penh and Siem Reap is currently being built with Japanese aid.

This leaves air and river transport as the only options for speedy travel around the country. Flights to Siem Reap from the capital take just 30 minutes. You can also take an express boat up the Tonlé Sap river and across the Tonlé Sap lake to Phnom Krom, from where you can hire a taxi to Siem Reap. It's an enjoyable 4-hour ride, although when the water is low during the dry season and smaller speedboats have to be used, it can also be a rather hair-raising one as well.

The most practical and inexpensive way to get around town is by *moto*, a two-seater motorcycle taxi. The *cyclo*, or cycle-rickshaw, is a slower, but more traditional South-East Asian mode of transport. There are some taxi cars available, especially at the airports. If you prefer to use one of these at other times, ask your hotel desk to arrange one for you.

Safety

Cambodia is now a country at peace, although at certain times —such as during elections— things might still get out of hand. Visitors will generally find, however, that Cambodians are friendly and helpful towards them. This doesn't mean that precautions shouldn't be taken. In Phnom Penh especially, make sure valuables, passports etc are kept in the hotel safe. Carry cash and travellers cheques in a money belt or sealable pocket, and be especially vigilant in crowded places where pickpockets operate, such as busy tourist sites. Be careful not to stray too far off the beaten track alone at night. And above all, if you're out in the countryside— including the area around the temples at Angkor—be aware that landmines laid by the Khmer Rouge rebels up to the mid-1990s are still a problem. Keep to designated paths, and never wander off into the jungle without a guide.

Time

Standard time in Cambodia is GMT+7, all year round.

Tipping

While tipping isn't customary in Cambodia, you should bear in mind that wages are extremely low and a tip for good service will be highly appreciated by the recipient.

Toilets

You won't find many public toilets on your travels around the country, so whenever you're in tourist-friendly places such as cafés, restaurants, hotels and museums, remember to take advantage of the facilities before you leave.

Tourist Information Offices

Tourist offices in Cambodia are not exactly packed with information. You might be able to elicit answers to basic questions about the country, but you're likely to come away knowing as much as when you went in. The tourist office at Pochentong Airport should be able to offer help about accommodation on arrival.

Voltage

Electric current is generally 220V, 50 cycle A.C., and sockets are for plugs with two round pins. Note that there power cuts can be frequent, although most of the larger hotels now have back-up generators. Bring a torch just in case.

INDEX

Airports 130
Angkor procedures 123
Angkor Thom 120–121
  Baphuon 121
  Bayon 120–121
  Royal Palace 121
Angkor Wat 119–120
Banteay Kdei 122
Banteay Srei 124
Battambang 126
Climate 130
Communications 130–131
Dining out 128–129
Driving 131
Emergencies 131
Festivals 132
Formalities 131
Health 131–132
History 109–112
Holidays 132
Kobal Spean 124
Kratie 125
Language 132–133
Media 133
Mekong Island 118
Money matters 133
Neak Pean 122
Opening hours 134
Phnom Bakheng 123
Phnom Chisor 118
Phnom Kulen 124
Phnom Penh 113–117
Central Market 116
Central Phnom Penh 115–117
  Colonial Quarter 117
  Independence Monument 116
  Killing Fields of Choeung Ek 117
  National Museum 115
  Palace quarter 113–114
  Royal Palace 114
  Sisowath Quay 116
  Tuol Sleng Museum 117
  Wat Ounalom 116
  Wat Phnom 116
Phnom Sampau 126
Photography 134
Prasat Kravan 122
Preah Khan 122
Public transport 134
Ream National Park 125
Roluos Group 123
Safety 135
Shopping 127
Sihanoukville 125
Ta Prohm 122
Time 135
Tipping 135
Toilets 135
Tonlé Bati 118
Tourist Information Offices 135
Udong 118
Voltage 135
Wat Banan 126

GENERAL EDITOR
  Barbara Ender-Jones
LAYOUT
  André Misteli
PHOTO CREDITS
  Renata Holzbachová:
  pp. 1, 25;
  Hémisphères/Boisberranger:
  pp. 3, 22;
  Hémisphères/Verdeil:
  pp. 4, 11, 17;
  Hémisphères/Cintract: p. 20
MAPS
  Elsner & Schichor
  JPM Publications

Copyright © 2005, 2002
by JPM Publications S.A.
12, avenue William-Fraisse,
1006 Lausanne, Switzerland
E-mail:
information@jpmguides.com
Web site:
http://www.jpmguides.com/

Printed in Switzerland
Weber/Bienne (CTP) — 04/10/01
Edition 2005